Exploring Spiritual Direction

Exploring Spiritual Direction

AN ESSAY ON
CHRISTIAN FRIENDSHIP

ALAN JONES

Harper & Row, Publishers, San Francisco
Cambridge, Hagerstown, New York, Philadelphia
London, Mexico City, São Paulo, Singapore, Sydney

For the students and faculty
of the General Theological Seminary:
guides, companions, and friends.

Note to the Reader
All biblical references are to the Revised Standard
Version of the Bible. Old Testament Section, copyright
© 1952; New Testament Section, First Edition, copyright
© 1946; Second Edition © 1971 by Division of Christian
Education of the National Council of Churches of Christ
in the United States of America.

Cover design: John Murello

Library of Congress Catalog Card Number: 81-18420
ISBN: 0-86683-782-5   (previously ISBN: 0-8164-2483-7)

Printed in the United States of America
87 88 89 90 11 10 9 8 7 6 5 4 3 2

Winston Press, Inc.
430 Oak Grove
Minneapolis, Minnesota 55403

Contents

Foreword

Books often begin with a "without whom . . ." paragraph in which the author acknowledges his indebtedness to those who were particularly helpful to him in the writing of his book. In the case of a book on companionship, a "without whom . . ." paragraph is indispensable. It would be impossible, however, to name all the companions who have affected me, but these in particular have influenced me deeply. They are Mary Coehlo, my colleague at the Center for Christian Spirituality; Ledlie Laughlin, rector of St. Luke's in the Fields, New York City; and James Fenhagen, the dean of the General Theological Seminary.

This book would not have been published without the encouragement of Avery Brooke or the patient supervision of the typing of the manuscript by Connie McPherson.

The Feast of the Transfiguration, 1981

Preface
The Art of Arts

Love one another as I have loved you.
(John 15:12)

Our culture tends to assume that unrestricted growth is desirable in every department of life. Just as businesses are expected to grow, so we want our lives to be more and more fulfilling. We easily come to believe that growth in its various forms is something that is ours by right.

The truth is that spiritual growth is not like economic expansion. It operates from a different set of assumptions. These assumptions spring from deep convictions with regard to the way in which God works in the world. The Christian belief that God loves us is deceptively simple. It means that God is actively seeking us out and wanting to be with us. And so spiritual growth is concerned with companionship: first, companionship with God, and second, companionship with our fellow human beings.

In part, the issue of companionship is the concern of the ancient practice of spiritual direction, but spiritual direction is something of a lost art. This book is a contribution to the efforts being made to revive it. I have tried to teach this subject in a seminary for nearly ten years; what I have set down in the following chapters are my reflections on my experience of struggling to understand the tradition of this art of arts and to pass it on to others.

The art of spiritual direction is rooted in two basic convictions. The first is that our relationship with God is of primary and fundamental importance. Without a sense of connection with God, all other relationships are impoverished. The second is that our relationship with God is bound up with our relationship with one another and with the whole created order. Sometimes our energies will be focused almost exclusively in one or other of these points of reference. At certain periods of our lives the sense of connection with God (what is sometimes called the vertical dimension) is all we have to pull us through a difficult time. At other periods we are called upon to concentrate on our relationships with others (what is sometimes called the horizontal dimension). Both are necessary. Each is related to the other and it is no accident that the horizontal and the vertical, when placed together, form a cross. It is that saving symbol that illuminates all attempts at spiritual guidance.

The pitfalls and surprises encountered in trying to teach spiritual direction are many. In a sense, it is unteachable. Certain themes, however, come up over and over again: God touching us through the agency of another when we least expect it and (wonderfully) when we least deserve it; finding that the vertical relation to God is both relaxing and challenging at the same time; being amazed by the gracious deference of God in using frail human instruments as agents of his purpose and his love.

In teaching this subject I have been struck by two things. The first is the enormous effort we put into frustrating and avoiding the very things for which we long. There seems to be no end to our facility for self-deception. That is why I need a spiritual guide to keep me honest. The second thing which has struck me over and over again is the wonderful miracle of God's transforming love, which, through the agency of another, is always drawing me out of myself and into a wider relationship with him. I have, therefore, been guided towards a rigorous honesty (because of my capacity for self-deception) and a firm hope (because of the transforming power of God's love) in struggling with this subject.

W. H. Auden says somewhere that life is a very grand opera played by a tenth-rate touring company. There is a double truth there which helps me understand the art of spiritual direction. It is, at once, sublime and ordinary, even funny. It requires a breadth of vision informed by a strict regard for reality. Peter Brook, one of the most creative and distinguished stage directors of this century, in his book *The Empty Space*, writes:

There are two ways of speaking about the human condition: there is the process of inspiration—by which all the positive elements can be revealed, and there is the process of honest vision—by which the artist bears witness to whatever it is that he has seen. The first process depends on revelation; it can't be brought about by holy wishes. The second one depends on honesty, and it mustn't be clouded over by holy wishes.[1]

Revelation and honesty give shape to spiritual companionship. It rests on revelation: revelation of God in Christ who continually calls us in the power of the Spirit into relationship with him. It rests on honesty: honesty with regard to what is there to be seen and to be reckoned with. To put it another way, spiritual companionship is a process of both nurture and confrontation.

It is this double aspect of spiritual guidance as both gift and demand which make the teaching of it possible. Both the teacher and the student are caught up in a common hope and submit to a common obedience. I have often had the tables turned on me in finding myself in the position of student rather than teacher. It is then that I have been caught by the miracle which no teaching can capture: friendship with others in God.

I have used the terms spiritual director and spiritual friend interchangeably. This has been deliberate, although done with considerable hesitation. The reason I have done so is to get across the idea that spiritual direction is not a peculiar or esoteric art, but one that is fundamental to ordinary human intercourse. Many people are put off by the term spiritual direction. It sounds formal and intimidating. It implies that we are to submit ourselves to another's judgment in an unreflective and unquestioning way. We may be willing to admit that our lives could do with a shift in direction, but the last thing we want to do is to be like soft wax in the hands of another to be shaped and molded according to his or her specifications.

St. Clement of Alexandria (c.150–c.215) wrote, "It is an absolute necessity that you who are haughty and powerful and rich should appoint for yourself some man as trainer and pilot. Let there be at all events one whom you respect, one whom you fear, one whom you accustom yourself to listen to when he is outspoken and severe, though all the while at your service."[2] St. Clement's admonition is both challenging and unattractive and he represents a strand in the tradition which I find enormously difficult. Nevertheless, there have been times in my life when a trainer or pilot was just what I needed. My overall conviction, however, is that such a relationship of submission, while necessary at times, is fraught with danger. As V. A. Demant put it, "All the authorities lay it down that a spiritual director must be experienced and wise, and ready to detach the disciple from dependence upon the director and so learn to stand on his own."[3] When we are being guided by a person who is more experienced that we are, it is appropriate to describe the relationship as one of spiritual direction. It is good, particularly as beginners, to sit at the feet of someone who is steeped in the mystical tradition. But I don't think that this "sitting at the feet" of another is meant to be a permanent arrangement. God has a way of sometimes reversing the role in spiritual direction so that the pupil teaches the master.

While I am not always sure I need a director, I do know that I need friends. I do, however, want to insist that spiritual direction is an ancient and noble art that should not be treated in the cavalier way we tend to treat friendship. The remedy is to take our friendships more seriously than we do rather than insist on a qualitative difference between direction and friendship.

Spiritual direction is a relationship entered into with another under mutual obedience to the revelation of God in Christ. No relationship is static, and all our relationships, insofar as they are under the guidance of the Holy Spirit, move more and more towards spiritual friendship. They move in that direction simply because this is the kind of God Christians believe in. Aelred of Rievaulx (1109–1167) put it very simply: "*Deus est amicitia.*" God is friendship. We are made after his image. And because of this, all our relationships carry within them the possibility of an ever-deepening intimacy in God.

My view of spiritual direction, therefore, is the result of an encounter between my own experience and the Christian tradition and the way in which the latter has stretched, challenged, and nurtured the former. Some of what I have to say may be idiosyncratic, but I trust that, insofar as my experience is interpreted and shaped by a common tradition, it will connect with that of others

on the same pilgrimage. Two personal stories may help to illuminate my understanding of this art of arts. The first tells how I first
received spiritual direction, the second, how I first became a spiritual director. Both stories point to the necessity of human companionship if there is to be spiritual growth.

I first came into contact with a spiritual director in my early
twenties and my initial experience of spiritual direction was one
of rescue. I was a confused and rebellious Christian drawn into
the fellowship of the Church in the hope that what was preached
might possibly be true. I was then a seminarian at the College
of the Resurrection where young men were trained for the priesthood in a monastic context. The college is situated in the bleak but
beautiful landscape of the Yorkshire moors in the north of England. I had come to Mirfield (as the college is often called after the
small town where it is situated) because I wanted to experience the
Christian life in what I thought would be its extreme form. I
thought the extremity of monasticism would help me see not only
if Christianity was real, but if I was.

I had never experienced such isolation. In the winter the stars
were still shining when we went to morning chapel and there
seemed to be nothing between me and the glittering heavens. I
experienced that wonder and terror of infinite space of which
Pascal speaks. My me began to disintegrate, not in the benign
disintegration of a person in the act of loving self-surrender. Mine
was the kind of dissolution that placed everything on quicksand. I
did not so much doubt God as I doubted myself. I even doubted
my doubts. I felt rather like the hero in Graham Greene's *The End
of the Affair*, which is the story "of a man who was . . . driven and
overwhelmed by the accumulation of natural coincidences, until he
broke and began to accept the incredible—the possibility of God."[4]
Greene intended the coincidences to continue over the years, forcing his hero to doubt his own atheism. This was precisely my own
experience. I needed rescuing from myself.

Rescue came in two ways, ways which have left an indelible
impression on me as signs of the gracious availability of God even
in the worst of times. The first was the sustaining power of a
worshipping, compassionate, and believing community. For a while
I was carried by the lively tradition of the Church, by the liturgical

rhythm of the community, and the compassionate presence of my fellow Christians. For a few weeks, then, I was sustained by the faith and faithfulness of the Christian community at a time when I felt that I had no faith at all or, rather, I felt that there was no "I" to have faith. Ever since then my favorite miracle story in the gospels is the one where the four friends of a man too sick to help himself opened up the roof of a house and lowered him on his bed and placed him at the feet of Jesus (Mark 2: 1–5). "When Jesus saw their faith, he said to the paralytic man, 'My son, your sins are forgiven.' " It was his friends' faith and not his own that saved him. I have always been impressed by the wonderful way in which we are able to carry one another, from time to time, in the Christian journey. It was small acts of love, not intellectual arguments, which began the process of breaking up the cloud of doubt that paralyzed me. I came to believe that my brand of atheism was a "crutch for those who could not bear the reality of God."[5]

The second part of the rescue operation was a summons from the dean of the seminary to go for an afternoon walk with him across the moors. I had no choice; walks with the dean (or principal as he was called) were part of a seminarian's lot. He was an extraordinary and powerful personality. I have since come to realize that he is an extremely complex man whose own psychological and spiritual wounds helped to make him the man he was and is. At the time I had no real notion of his own hurts. I received nothing but receptivity and love and it was this which influenced me deeply. It was as if he could see into my deepest self. He was able to show me that God loved me all the way through. He was the bearer of the miracle that I mattered. This doctrine that I matter, that people matter, was and is the hardest thing for me to believe. My struggle with other aspects of Christian belief are insignificant compared with the difficulty I have in accepting that I am loved.

My walk with the principal across the moors was one of the many incidents that convinced me that I was loved, and it was this that continued the healing process of breaking up the cloud of doubt that had paralyzed me. Aelred wrote of this fundamental experience in *The Mirror of Love*:

And those men who were around me, but who were ignorant of the things which went on within me, kept saying, "how lucky he is, how lucky he is." But they did not know that there was evil in me, where only good should be. Terrible was the distress I felt within myself, tormenting me, corrupting my soul with intolerable stench. And unless you had quickly stretched out your hand, not being able to tolerate myself, I might have taken the most desperate remedy of despair.[6]

Thus, my first experience of spiritual direction was one of rescue. Someone stretched out his hand to me at a time when I couldn't tolerate myself. I was touched by another in the fellowship of the Church and told (not in words) that I mattered. That is what brought me to Christianity and keeps me Christian: the miracle that I matter. This conviction came to me only through the agency of others and was regarded as commonplace in the Catholic (Anglican) tradition in which I was trained. It was taken for granted that we should seek spiritual direction in a regular and disciplined way because the journey was sometimes difficult and even dangerous. We students were reminded of the words of St. Cyril of Jerusalem (c.315–c.386) to his catechumens: "The dragon sits by the side of the road, watching those who pass. Beware lest he devour you. We go to the Father of Souls, but it is necessary to pass by the dragon."

Does this sound rather melodramatic? I don't think it is. There are dragons to be encountered along life's journey and that is why direction, guidance, and companionship are so important. I needed in my early twenties—and I still need—to be taken up by someone and shown the way. It is this experience of being taken up that I find graceful. But is it spiritual direction? It is, I think, when one is trying to walk the Way of Christ. Those who have taken me up assumed there was a Way, a direction in which to walk, and I value and treasure those relationships, both formal and informal, which have continually set my feet on the right path when I was lost.

But how did I become a spiritual director? How can anyone presume to become a director of souls? The beginnings of an answer was given in the telling of my experiences in seminary. Becoming a spiritual director depends on the following of a Way that is open before you and that has already been well-trodden. The director is not alone. He or she stands within a tradition and with a great company. Nevertheless, I was mesmerized by the enormity of the vocation. It was, at once, alarming and seductive: alarming, because of a sense of inadequacy; seductive, because of the possibility of acquiring power over others. The director is in great danger from both sides. A sense of inadequacy can rob the director of the proper sense of confidence in God that true direction demands. A grasping for power can lead to serious consequences for both the director and those seeking guidance.

The first person to formally ask me to be his spiritual director did a great deal both to give me confidence and to undermine any notion that the power was mine. He was a monk, more than twice my age, who was a renowned scholar and acknowledged by his brothers to be saintly, if somewhat eccentric. He was a man of deep prayer. The absurdity of his asking me to be his spiritual director was overwhelming. My conversation with him went something like this:

> Alan, I want you to be my spiritual director.
> (Laughing) But brother, I can't!
> (with a twinkle in his eye) I know!

This monk knew three things I needed to learn. The first was that people need direction from time to time. The second was that my incompetence need not be an impediment as long as I didn't rely on my own limited resources. The third was that the true director of us both was the Holy Spirit on whom we both waited expectantly.

These two experiences (the first of being rescued, the second of being trusted) have colored my view of spiritual direction ever since. There is also a third kind of experience which has often given me a sense of inner direction, and that is my encounter with the minds of others through their writing. Particular authors are too numerous to mention, but their works range from the scriptures themselves to those of modern fiction. The point is that I find that some writers have the knack of intervening in—and even interfering with—my sense of reality. Such writers act as spiritual companions.

Robert Coles, in describing the work of Flannery O'Connor,

writes that human beings need occasional intervention from outside which "impinges directly, severely, on their sense of self. It is an intervention that entails humiliation and loss, a subsequent erosion of that cocksure moralizing inclination [that] sets the stage for a possible gain—the mind a bit cleaner, a bit less self-deluded."[7]

I use Flannery O'Connor as an example because I find her writing extremely difficult and her persistent refusal to give her readers anyone to admire in her stories hard to take. She throws me back on myself and invites me to ask disturbing questions. She helps me in my waiting for God, which is no easier now than it was twenty years ago when I walked on the Yorkshire moors. The difference now is that in my forties waiting for God and the Christian pattern of self-abandonment to the love of God are much closer to the heart of things as I understand them.

What do I look for in a spiritual director now? The element of rescue hasn't completely disappeared, but there is now a stronger sense of need for simple companionship, for spiritual friendship. I become less interested in the popular demand for self-affirmation than in the need for the development of a strenuous honesty about myself: a self who can stand being scrutinized because he knows he is loved.

The friends I value most are those who love me unreservedly but with discrimination. They are willing to scrutinize me. They make their presence felt. They make a difference. Graham Greene beautifully describes the benign influence of his friend Herbert Reed. He "would come into a room full of people and you wouldn't notice his coming—you noticed only that the whole atmosphere of a discussion had quietly altered, that even the relations of one guest with another had changed. No one any longer would be talking for effect, and when you looked around for an explanation there he was—complete honesty born of complete experience had entered the room and unobtrusively taken a chair."[8]

In describing the work of Flannery O'Connor, Robert Coles shows me what I look for in a spiritual companion. No doubt I will grow and change as much in the next twenty years as I have in the past. I certainly hope so. Meanwhile, here in the middle of the pilgrimage is what speaks to me.

She wrote . . . for herself, for those she knew and loved, for any of us, who care to stop and look and listen. She wrote in the wish that she, that her readers, might be granted a moment or longer of surcease from ourselves, that we might transcend what we're called or considered, a Yankee this or a southern that, and instead become the property of Another, of Someone who long ago indicated His impatience with the various categorizations we use to put people in various places. She was herself a southern intellectual, a writer with few peers in the recent American past, and a writer, also, of enormous promise, taken from us far too soon. But finally, one believes, she was a soul blinded by faith; hence, with an uncanny endowment of sight. She had a large smile. She had the generosity of one who wanted company along a tough but extremely important journey; . .[9]

That is what I want too: company along a tough but extremely important journey.

It is in this spirit of gratitude and the need for companionship that the following chapters are offered to my fellow pilgrims.

1

Spiritual Warfare and the Need for Companionship

Finally, be strong in the Lord and in the strength of his might. Put on the whole armor of God, that you may be able to stand against the wiles of the devil. For we are not contending against flesh and blood, but against the principalities, against the powers, against the world rulers of this present darkness, against the spiritual hosts of wickedness in the heavenly places. Therefore take the whole armor of God, that you may be able to withstand in the evil day, and having done all, to stand. Stand therefore, having girded your loins with truth, and having put on the breast-plate of righteousness, and having shod your feet with the equipment of the gospel of peace; above all taking the shield of faith, with which you can quench all the flaming darts of the evil one. And take the helmet of salvation, and the sword of the Spirit, which is the word of God. Pray at all times in the Spirit, with all prayer and supplication.

Ephesians 6: 10–18

The Christian life has often been depicted as a warfare against terrible inner destructive forces. One immediately thinks of John Bunyan's *Pilgrim's Progress* where we read of Christian's departure from the City of Destruction and of his subsequent struggles, temptations, and triumphs. Christian has to do battle with Apollyon, the destroyer.

Then Apollyon, espying his opportunity, began to gather up close to Christian, and wrestling with him, gave him a dreadful fall; and with that Christian's sword flew out of his hand. Then said Appolyon, "I am sure of thee now," and with that he had

almost pressed him to death, so that Christian began to despair
of life. But as God would have it, while Apollyon was fetching
of his last blow thereby to make a full end of this good man,
Christian nimbly reached out his hand for his sword, and caught
it, saying "Rejoice not against me, O mine enemy! when I fall I
shall arise," and with that gave him a deadly thrust, which made
him give back as one that had received his mortal wound: Christian perceiving that, made at him again, saying, "Nay, in all these
things we are more than conquerors through him that loved us."
And with that Apollyon spread forth his dragon's wings, and sped
him away, that Christian saw him no more.[1]

This metaphor of battle needs to be revived today because the
world in which we live is in a peculiar state of crisis and upheaval.
Apollyon still walks the earth. Life is always uncertain, but our age
is characterized by an unusually high level of instability. Our anxiety about security and authority pushes us into seeing life more and
more as a struggle, and in such a situation our need for guidance
and companionship is intensified.

Problems arise, however, when we choose one metaphor over
another to describe the Christian life. With the metaphor of battle,
two particular problems come to mind. The first is that human
beings in times of crisis like an easily identifiable enemy. The
second is that when an enemy has been overcome, we are puffed
up by the illusion of our own power. Both problems point to the
need for companionship, guidance, and direction.

Whenever we are threatened we tend to divide the world up, in
a facile way, between the good guys and the bad guys. In the
Christian battle the enemy is far too subtle a foe to be so easily
identified. It is easy to see wickedness, sin, and evil all around,
especially in obvious places where sex, money, or power are the
predominant themes. But the battle of which we speak, while
sometimes involving the obvious and blatant sins, is waged on a far
deeper level than mere conventional wrongdoing.

We are attracted to the holy and we disbelieve in it at the same
time. Faith is sometimes a struggle and belief is often hard. The
enemy, then, is not easily identifiable because our struggle is often
an interior one. Admittedly there are Christians who claim that
faith is easy. Problems dissolve in the face of firm belief. I am

genuinely puzzled by such an assertion because it nowhere connects with my experience or with my reading of the human drama. I believe that our life is both a longing for and a struggle with holiness.

Our God reveals himself as holy: "Holy, Holy, Holy, Lord God of Hosts: Heaven and earth are full of your glory." Once we begin to believe this our life becomes shaped by a feeling of awe, a sense of radical amazement. When Moses was confronted by the holiness of God in the burning bush, his life was changed. Holiness means life in God. It involves the movement towards integrity in our living and loving. It is a way of talking about the primacy of that vertical relationship between God and each of us which undergirds and shapes all our other relationships. Theophilous of Antioch (late second century) wrote, "Show me your man and I will show you my God," which is another way of saying that human life, to be truly human, is meant to be bound up in the life of God. Why then do I sometimes identify that which is my very life as my enemy? Why do I often refuse to pay attention to the law of my own being? It is at such moments that I value the wisdom and companionship of another. I need, from time to time, the disarming and probing mind of a spiritual director who will help me see who my true friends are and who are my real enemies in my interior life. A spiritual guide helps me pay attention to the biblical imperative: "Be holy; for I the Lord your God am holy" (Lev. 19:2).

The Christian battle, therefore, is not merely a fight against the destructive darkness in the world and in ourselves, it is also a battle for and towards a fuller and more abundant life. It concerns our destiny in the loving holiness of God. Above all, it is a battle in which the decisive victory has already been won by Christ on the cross. The enemy is anything that eats away at our humanity both individually and collectively: our resentments, our prejudices, our collective greed, and our unnamed fears. There are often deeper enemies behind the conventional ones of sex, money, and power. The latter, after all, are often little more than seductive narcotics to dull the pain of our disappointments and unsatisfied longings. Deeper forms of wickedness can be perpetrated by righteous people who are publicly committed to the fostering of spiritual and moral values. We may find that what we thought was a terrible enemy within is, in reality, a wonderful ally. Even the reverse can be true. What we think of as a strength may, in fact, be the source of our greatest weakness. Often we can't tell the difference between the good and the bad things that happen to us until many years after the events. In time, our interpretation of them changes so that what seemed a bad or even tragic happening ten years ago, is now seen, in retrospect, as having good results because it stretched us and made us grow. This is just as true for communities as it is for individuals.

The enemy, then, is not always easily identifiable. That is why the Christian life requires our discovering criteria for discernment and our seeking the direction and guidance of the Holy Spirit. This guidance is available to us in a relationship of spiritual direction. Without the ability to discern between the various forces at work in us we would be like an undisciplined athlete. St. Paul saw himself as a disciplined runner or a dedicated boxer:

> For my part, I run with a clear goal before me; I am like a boxer who does not beat the air; I bruise my own body and make it know its master, for fear that after preaching to others I should find myself rejected.
>
> I Cor. 9: 26, NEB

Without the guidance of the Spirit we will be tempted to fling ourselves into pointless activity, but never lead Christ-centered lives.

Christian discernment, as we shall see, requires Christian companionship because it involves us in the life of a discerning community. Criteria for discerning the root causes of our complex impulses and desires begin to emerge when we immerse ourselves in the life of a believing community. The Christian fellowship is formed by its attentiveness to the Christian drama as it unfolds in the reading of the scriptures and the celebration of the liturgy. Discernment, therefore, is a way of testing the dramatic shape of our own individual life against the great drama of God who continually calls us to himself. This drama is revealed in the Bible and celebrated in the Eucharist.

In the Eucharist is focused the double movement of attraction and repulsion with regard to holiness. We are attracted by the call into an intimate fellowship which the Eucharist signifies. We are repelled by the call to sacrifice which accompanies it. The call to sacrifice tempts one often to externalize the battle. I say to myself, "All my problems come to me from outside. All I want to do is to respond to the love of God which is always luring me. It is other people and external circumstances that keep disrupting my deepest wishes." At such times it is often a spiritual companion who calls my bluff. Without a spiritual director I get lost in a web of self-deception and even imagine that my little victories in the interior life are the result of my own inherent wisdom.

This brings us to the second problem with the metaphor of battle. Not only are we in danger of too easily identifying our enemies, we are also prey to the insidious belief that when an enemy has been overcome we have done it all by our own unaided efforts. We imagine that once an enemy has been suppressed it has gone forever. The spiritual battle then becomes our work, something we accomplish. When that happens all the sins that we associate with religious people come into focus: self-righteousness, moralism, and judgmentalism—which are the real enemies of the holy life for which we long.

Christian warfare, therefore, requires us to acknowledge our longing for God and our need for companionship. It also necessitates the belief that God really loves us and that Christ won a final and decisive victory over all that would destroy us. It is only in this context of faith that Christian discipline makes any sense. Christian discipline is simply a means of opening ourselves more and more fully to the energy of God's love: an energy that informs our faith and enables us to get through those times when belief is an agonizing struggle. It is at such times that we need the supporting hand of a fellow pilgrim.

In this context the image of battle with regard to the Christian life is a challenging and exciting one. It is one that peculiarly suits the movements of our time. There are signs of a new religious revivalism that has taken the more traditional churches by surprise. People are dissatisfied with an easy, undemanding, and unchallenging form of religious commitment. The principle seems to be strict churches grow while permissive churches contract. This is by no means a bad thing. The question is what things do we wish to be strict about? Again this raises the issue of discernment. A religion that fails to elicit serious life-and-death commitment in its adherents is worthless, but the kind of strictness that we see in much revivalism today can lead to a sentimental shallowness and gross oversimplification. As one commentator put it recently:

> The return-to-strictness aspect can lead to anything from a distorting sexual denial and a blearing of intellectual clarity to, at its horrendous worst, the totalitarianism of the spirit which produced the mass-suicide at Jonestown in Guyana in 1978. That happens because a period of innovation and experimentation is a magnet to the bad as well as the good, the weak as well as the strong. But the aberrations and distortions, in both Christendom and Islam, should not conceal the essence of what is happening: which is that a stubbornly renewed demand for access to nonmaterial values is generating the supply to meet that demand.[2]

There is a battle raging whether we acknowledge it or not; it is a battle for the hearts of men and women. It is a struggle for the jaundiced souls of those who "have grown up to assume that life is externally about the efficient or compassionate management of rapid technical change and internally about the rational explaining away (or whisky-and-valium stupefying) of private unhappiness."[3] The Christian gospel proclaims that the private unhappiness infecting our interior life cannot be dealt with solely by the application of various therapeutic and spiritual techniques. Still less can the problems of our life with others in society be dealt with by the application of a spiritual technology. This is not to say that skills and techniques are not important, but rather to point out that the deeper battles of the human spirit concern our basic longings and allegiances.

This is an added reason why spiritual guidance is necessary in an age when men and women are nagged by uncertainties. When we are wracked by doubt we are ripe for a message of rigid certainty. The marketplace is full of religious practitioners who are ready to exploit our anxieties, fears, and prejudices. The battle, then, is a serious one, and the stakes are high.

This brings us to the heart of the problem with regard to any form of spiritual guidance. It lends itself easily to abuse. People require guidance. The question is how can we submit ourselves to the judgment of another and avoid the pitfalls of exploitation and abuse? Guidance presupposes a willingness to submit to the judgment of another, to acknowledge that he or she knows best. No matter how one tries to cover it up, spiritual direction is based on both submission and obedience. That is why the Christian tradition insists that the director be a person of considerable self-knowledge rooted in a life of penitence and prayer. The relationship is grounded in a common obedience to the third always present in any human encounter. As Aelred puts it at the beginning of his treatise on friendship: "Here we are, you and I, and I hope a third, Christ, is in our midst."[4]

In spite of the allegiance to Christ which the director and the directed share, exploitation is always a possibility and a temptation. Our hunger for God is such that we will go to any lengths either to satisfy or repress it. We long for guidance. We like the clear voice of authority. We like to feel that we belong.

A strong and growing Church, ready to do the battle, is one of high commitment, strong loyalties, and missionary zeal. But there is the frightening possibility of intolerance, absolutist demands, and unbending dogmatism taking over. People of deep religious convictions are as much prey to spiritual and psychological tyrannies as anyone else. It is precisely among those who take the spiritual life seriously that the greatest danger lies. C. S. Lewis wrote wittily in *The Screwtape Letters* of the way the devil is able to exploit our religious impulses, and there is a warning in St. Matthew's gospel about mere spiritual gymnastics.

> When the unclean spirit has gone out of a man, he passes through waterless places seeking rest, but he finds none. Then he says, 'I will return to my house from which I came.' And when he comes he finds it empty, swept, and put in order. Then he goes and brings with him seven other spirits more evil than himself, and they enter and dwell there; and the last state of that man becomes worse than the first. So shall it be also with this evil generation.
> Matt. 12: 43–45

Often our battle will seem unspectacular. We may have to fight against a dreariness of spirit which, when it is driven out, leaves us relieved but empty. The human heart desires and needs to be possessed. A strong affection or ruling love must fill the vacancy. Our being able to welcome into our lives the Spirit of God is the critical moment of liberty in the battle for the human heart. What this gospel passage tells us is that unless we are vigilant it is as possible to grow worse as it is to grow better. Our lives are strewn with wasted opportunities and unused victories, and the battle is never ending for our allegiance.

Consciously or unconsciously, as the years go by, all of us more and more submit ourselves to some allegiance and our spirit and intellect are brought into captivity to some obedience. For better or worse, things that seemed difficult or impossible a few years ago will come almost naturally to us a few years later. We will have become accustomed to take a certain course, to obey certain impulses. We are, after all, creatures of habit.

But what is our primary allegiance? First, we may be giving our allegiance more and more to the love of self in its various forms. Or we may be surrendering more and more to the love of God— albeit falteringly, and with many struggles and failures, but, nevertheless, truly and faithfully. Third, we may be like the person in Matthew who has struggled and triumphed but remains vacant. But the heart cannot live without allegiance, without surrender. We may, for a while, sit on the fence, balanced between one love and the other, but the equilibrium is uneasy and does not last. In the end we have to choose. If we do not ourselves choose, others will make our choices for us.

In the ensuing battle concerning our life's allegiances, we must not fall into the trap of negativity. The battle is not so much for the uprooting of evil (although it is that), but rather for the opening up to the loving and healing work of the Spirit. We are often tempted to underestimate the spiritual resources and capacities of human beings and, therefore, to deny the power and grace of God working and struggling in us. A human being is a longing for God and nothing less than God will satisfy us; the seductive voices that would make us anything less than this are to be resisted. Our battle will continually be with the deadly reductionisms in the world today; with attitudes that diminish human beings to disposable commodities, to means to commercial or political ends.

Perhaps the hardest requirement in the Christian battle is patience. Often it all seems too unspectacular and painfully slow. It is hard to wait in the face of so much human suffering and need. We want results and we want them now, but God's successes are always ahead of us in the future where we cannot always see them. The battle, then, is concerned with our "choosing God" in patience and in faith. As we have seen, to do this we need the fellowship of the Christian community and the accumulated wisdom of the Christian tradition. We shall also be armored against pessimism and negativity if we cultivate one simple virtue: delight in and gratitude for existence. The battle loses its deadly grimness if we learn the art of giving thanks. Without this sense of gratitude the discipline becomes burdensome and boring. St. Matthew's gospel insists on the lightness of the yoke.

> Take my yoke upon you, and learn from me; for I am gentle and lowly in heart, and you will find rest for your souls. For my yoke is easy, and my burden is light.
>
> Matt. 11: 29–30

G. K. Chesterton manifested this one virtue, gratitude for existence, when he wrote:

> You say grace before meals.
> All right.
> But I say grace before the play and the opera,
> And grace before the concert and pantomime,
> And grace before I open a book,
> And grace before sketching and painting,
> Swimming, fencing, boxing, walking, playing, dancing;
> And grace before I dip pen in the ink.[5]

Gratitude is the first step towards true discernment in the spiritual battle because it opens us up and makes us receptive to God's action in us.

In Dante's *Divine Comedy*, hell is reserved for those who have "lost the good of intellect." Dante doesn't mean that hell is for the stupid and heaven is only for intellectuals. By intellect he means the discerning, intuitive center of the human being. It is the faculty that enables us to relate to God and that makes us fundamentally and truly human. It is, for Dante, the organ of discrimination, of discretion that enables us to discern the right relationship things have one with another. When this faculty to discern true from false relationships is impaired, life becomes hellish.

The modern equivalent of this Dantean anti-intellectual mindset cultivates moral confusion by robbing us of the organ of discernment. We need "law and order" if we are to live freely, but discernment is necessary if we are to tell the difference between law and order which is repressive and totalitarian, and law and order which is a manifestation of the ordering of God's love for us. All our struggling in the Christian life is for the right ordering of our lives so that we may love more fully and openly. Christian discipline is concerned with the directions and harnessing of all our energies of love. Our purpose, like Dante's, is not to dwell on the miseries of hell, but to bring us to heaven. The movement between the two, however, requires us to believe that we are truly free to move in one direction or another. If it is possible to progress, it is also possible to regress. If the good news is that we are found in Christ, it must also be true that being lost is a real possibility.

The belief that we are truly free has been seriously eroded in our generation by a too hasty and often shallow application of the insights of psychology. Shallow psychologizing weakens our sense of freedom because we too easily see ourselves as victims of unconscious forces so that we can say boldly, "I am not responsible. It's not my fault," which is the same as saying, "The devil made me do it!" We tend to mortgage our freedom by blaming our actions on things outside us: "It's the environment; it's heredity; it's my glands." There is a litany of excuses which sing out when we are confronted with the terrible promise and possibility that we are free. If we are truly free, then we are free to engage seriously in the battle that fully human life inevitably offers. When I am free I am responsible for who I am and what I do. We are not slaves either to hormones or to chance. What we do matters and matters deeply.

Modern therapy, at its best, can help us prepare for a deeper and a more wonderful engagement with life, with its struggles and opportunities. It often begins with the dismantling of a false sense of self, and in order to do this old mechanisms that held that false self together have to be removed. These mechanisms enslave the

self, as do patterns of guilt, which keep us on a terrible treadmill—
the treadmill of compulsiveness masquerading as duty; the treadmill of self-absorption under the guise of self-expression; the
treadmill of moral confusion under the cloak of newness of life.
The therapeutic process of dismantling this old self brings the
patient into a place of moral openness where freedom seems to
be an "impossible dream." When this happens, the darker and
more important work of spiritual therapy is about to begin. This is
the work of recovering the sense of a true and responsible self by
asking the simple question: What are you going to do *now*? Now
that you've stopped blaming your mother, your father, your husband, your wife, your environment, the state of the nation, the
capitalist system, the communist one, your arthritis, etc., etc., etc.!
Sooner or later, to be fully human we have to be confronted with
a choice, because human life, in the end, is a matter of allegiance,
of obedience.

> And if you be unwilling to serve the Lord, choose this day whom
> you will serve, whether the gods your fathers served in the region
> beyond the River, or the gods of the Amorites in whose land you
> dwell; but as for me and my house, we will serve the Lord.
>
> Josh. 24: 15

The mature Christian life is a battle about choices and how we
make them in the face of temptation, suffering, and conflict. It is
also about the right use of the victories that God continually wins
in us and for us as we learn to choose freely his will for us which
is our peace. But there is war in heaven.

> Now war arose in heaven, Michael and his angels fighting against
> the dragon.
>
> Rev. 12: 7

The theme of spiritual warfare, war in heaven, which continues
to be waged in us and around us today, is the subject of a great
spiritual classic, *Spiritual Combat*, written by a priest, Lorenzo
Scupoli, in the sixteenth century. This work was translated into
Greek two centuries later under the title of *Unseen Warfare*, and
in the nineteenth century it found its way to Russia. In it are set
down the necessity and the conditions of the spiritual struggle. The

struggle is inevitable because the human race is off course and has lost its way. Discernment between good and evil is very important because the Christian call involves the development of a character that is willing to be purged of the latter and be cultivated in the former, and be then set back on the right path.

The spiritual armory for this unseen warfare consists of four simple precepts:

1. *Never rely on yourself in anything.* The writer encourages us to cultivate a healthy disbelief in ourselves not in a psychologically sick way but simply as a matter of fact. To put it simply, we need constantly to be reminded that we are not God! Not that anyone deliberately goes around thinking that he is, but rather that most of us live as if we are the originating center of events. Part of our formation as Christians is to struggle to live from the Center who is God and not from the center which is ourselves. The whole of life goes wrong when we are eccentric (off-center) and we need helps, guides, traditions, friends to help us get and keep on track.

2. *Bear always in your heart a perfect and all-daring trust in God alone.* The second precept invites the Christian soldier to a wonderful naked trustfulness. The first precept without the second would be an invitation to despair. A battle cannot be waged without a strong hope and a sure confidence. The point is that we have none to rely on except God, and God can do all things.

The last two precepts are simply ways of keeping constantly in mind the first two.

3. *Strive without ceasing,* which means that there is hard work involved.

4. *Remain constantly in prayer,* which will act as a constant reminder that the work is God's.

All that is required, then, in the Christian battle is for us to remember who we are and who God is. Nothing could be simpler! Yet nothing is harder for human beings because we are forgetful, myopic, and ignorant. I easily forget God, I am short-sighted with regard to my relationship with him and with others, I am deeply ignorant of my own true self. And without the help of friends, communities, disciplines I cannot know God, myself, or others.

So the Christian program for creative nurturing survival is very simple. The armor is what it has always been: faith in and obedience to God. Our survival kit is simply an all-daring trust in God. But there are other survival kits on the market. There are, for example, many techniques available to us for psychological and material survival in this unsteady and inflationary age. It has been suggested, for example, that we each make our own survival kit of the following: a supply of canned sardines, a bicycle, a cache of South African gold coins, and a machine gun. That is one way of taking the battle of life frighteningly seriously. This particular kit is becoming increasingly popular. The terrible thing is that this survivalist mentality cuts us off from one another. We lose the sense of a common pilgrimage, a common destiny. Charles Moss, a retired highway engineer, fears the collapse of society so he hoards gold, silver, and grain. He also has several rifles and shotguns mostly for hunting but if necessary for shooting people. Mike McKinney, a former Los Angeles police officer, has a five-year supply of survival food and a cache of 100 weapons. "If you came to me with a month's worth of freeze-dried goods to trade to me for my M-IA rifle," he said, "I'd end up with both my M-IA and the food."[6]

The battle for sovereignty over the human heart, however, is of a different order. The making of a human being has nothing to do with gold coins or machine guns. The breaking of them does and that is why the battle is important.

There are no short cuts to the making of a human being. Our formation takes many years and this is because human beings don't just happen. We are made and re-made. In fact our becoming fully human depends on our willingness to respond to God's challenge to us to be more than we think we are. The heroes of Graham Greene's novels are often men struggling in search of their own souls. In his *Dr. Fischer of Geneva, or The Bomb Party*, he outlines the requirements necessary for a human being to have a soul. Greene's hero is talking with his young wife about her malicious father and his hideous friends. She begins with the strangely antiquated question: "Have you a soul?"

> "I think I may have one—shop-soiled but still there.
> If souls exist you certainly have one."
> "Why?"
> "You've suffered."[7]

Graham Greene's first requirement for our having a soul is the willingness to suffer for another. As unpalatable and unfashionable as this is, it is corroborated by the Christian mystical tradition. Indeed suffering is one of the major reasons why we avoid spiritual warfare and repress our hunger for God. It is not that we are to seek suffering, but rather that it is an inevitable part of serious engagement. And what is true for individuals is true for nations. André Gide, the French critic, wrote in the 1920s that America didn't deserve to have a soul because she had not yet plunged into the crucible of suffering. This is unfair with regard to the United States today but Gide's general point is an arresting one. Soul-making, both for individuals and peoples, involves suffering.

Monsieur Belmont (one of Dr. Fischer's friends) is a busy lawyer specializing in tax evasion. As for a soul "he hasn't the time to develop one. . . . A soul requires a private life. Belmont has no time for a private life." The second requirement, then, is a commitment to a life that is marked by moments of solitude. There can be no growth in the spirit without the willingness to enter into suffering should it come, and without a firm commitment to regular times of solitude for prayer and for simply waiting on God.

The Divisionnaire (a soldier) in the book, "might just possibly have a soul. There's something unhappy about him."

> "Is that always a sign?"
> "I think it is."
> "And Mr. Kips?"
> "I'm not sure about him either. There's a sense of disappointment about Mr. Kips. He might be looking for something he mislaid. Perhaps he's looking for his soul and not a dollar."[8]

Unhappiness and disappointment may seem strange requirements for the making of a soul and yet Greene's gloomy way of describing things is basically in tune with the theme of restlessness we find in the Christian tradition with regard to our longing for God. "Thou hast made us for thyself and our heart is restless until it finds its rest in thee." So St. Augustine gave voice to the deep restlessness in human beings. We have deep hungers within us which seem insatiable and often our unhappiness and disappointment are signs of our longing for God. When that is repressed our unhappiness and disappointment are prevented from becoming agents of transformation. Instead they become the cause of an ever-deepening sense of bitterness and resentment. But this is precisely where the battle is engaged in our struggle to discover what will satisfy our deepest longings. Self-satisfaction can have no place in the making of a human being, as Graham Greene here points out in his analysis of the last of his father-in-law's toadlike friends. Richard Deane is an aging movie idol.

> "No. Definitely not. No soul. I'm told he has copies of his old films and he plays them over every night to himself. He has no time even to read the books of the films. He's satisfied with himself. If you have a soul you can't be satisfied."[9]

There we have Graham Greene's three requirements for the making of a soul: the willingness to suffer for another, a commitment to moments of solitude, and a willingness to pay attention to our deep restlessness of spirit. But these three ingredients do not necessarily produce human beings who are commendable. Greene's hero's father-in-law fulfills all these requirements but he has no daring confidence in God.

> "And my father?"
> "He has a soul all right!" I said, "but I think it may be a damned one."[10]

Now all this talk of our having souls and of the possibility of damnation seems quaint and old-fashioned. There are, nevertheless, deep and abiding truths behind this language. When we talk about a human being having a soul we do not have to embrace an unacceptable philosophy which divides body and soul. It is simply a way of reviving the deep Christian conviction of the infinite value of every person. Damnation is a dark and difficult word but it too points to the fact that the stakes are high and the battle is serious. Our choices do matter and the issue of our final allegiance has consequences for eternity.

It is no wonder that I need all the help I can muster. I need the fellowship of the Christian community, the love of my family, the sustenance provided by the Bible, and the sacraments, if I am to grow. Without spiritual companionship I shrivel and die inside. Above all, I need a spiritual friend or group of friends of the soul who are able to see right through me and love me as I am.

There is a wonderful passage in Paul Scott's novel *The Towers of Silence* that describes the kind of friends for which I long. Barbara Batchelor is a retired and garrulous missionary in India. She is also a strong and wonderful human being underneath all her fuss and chatter. Sarah Layton is the only person in the book who has bothered to notice the glory under the surface. Barbara is grateful for Sarah's penetrating gaze.

> She looks at my old fond foolish face and sees through it, I think, sees below the ruination, hears behind the senseless, ceaseless chatter, sees right down to the despair but also beyond to the terrific thing there really is in me, the joy I would find in God and which she would find in life, which come to much the same thing.[11]

If I am to engage in this fantastic battle for my life-in-God, I need the compassion of my companions. I need someone who penetrates my senseless ceaseless chatter and sees the terrific thing there really is in me. This is a good definition of the ancient role of spiritual director or friend of the soul. He or she is one who enters the battle with me and, if necessary, fights against the me who is sometimes tempted by cynicism or despair. In the Christian Way we discover that we need not only to believe in God, but also to believe in each other. A spiritual director enters the lists on my behalf against the enemy within who would undermine my naked confidence in God. This friend of my soul is a bearer of good news. He or she, by simply staying by my side through difficult times, proclaims that I am more than my cynicism and despair. There is in me, after all, a terrific thing.

One of the oldest metaphors for the Church is a mighty army. It was an image particularly revered in the Middle Ages during the period of the Crusades. It is true that the Crusades brought out the worst as well as the best in human beings, but in spite of the desire for plunder and conquest, there was a genuine motive to free the Christian Holy Places from Islamic domination. In *St. Francis of Assisi* by Nikos Kazantzakis, St. Francis sees his mission in the world as a crusade against all that imprisons humankind. He is *miles Christi* (soldier of Christ) and we will end this chapter on warfare with this absurd image of St. Francis as a soldier. The picture of the wildly loving saint as a bedraggled and pathetic military figure will help us realize the kind of warfare in which we are engaged. With St. Francis as our model (and behind him, of course, the model of Christ himself) we will not be tempted to imitate the polemics and belligerence of the world, nor will we be seduced by popular forms of religious exploitation. God's strength in Christ is manifested in brokenness and weakness and this strange strength of the crucified God is also manifested in the raggedly dressed, fiery-eyed, crazed-with-love figure of St. Francis. This image sets the tone of the task of spiritual companionship: its seriousness, its humor, and its joy. It is for the freeing of the souls of men and women.[12]

In order for us to proceed and enter the battle we shall have to examine more deeply what it means to daringly trust God. Our full humanity is born out of our being able to accept our own fragile selves as a gift from God. A human being is God's handiwork and because of this we can begin with confidence. So many of us miss the point by failing to begin here with the sheer giftedness of it all. When we begin (and it often takes the unexpectedness of the insight of a friend who can discern the terrific thing there is in us) with our life as sheer gift we can then dare get ready for battle. We dare risk the painful discipline of self-examination without which there is no growth, no striving, no stretching of the mind and heart to receive God. Christian discipline is for the enlarging of the heart and our spiritual combat is solely for this purpose.

2

The Spiritual Supermarket
The Search for the Good and the Beautiful

S piritual guidance has to happen within the context of the actual world and take seriously actual conditions and events. This, of course, is obvious, but without this commonplace grounding, spiritual direction can become "spiritualized" and disconnected from everyday life. I must always begin with paying attention to what is *there* happening in life. To do this I need an active imagination in order to appreciate all that is going on. I also need a way of distancing myself from events so that I can see them in perspective. A spiritual friend is one who both stimulates the imagination and also helps me gain a critical distance from the main currents and events of my life so that I can take a fresh look at where I am and where I am going. This double process of imaging and distancing is very important if we are to help each other to grow. I want now to look at this double process and see how it leads us to a life of sacrifice and service which is at once freeing and delightful.

We live in a spiritual supermarket and before we examine the process of imaging and distancing it would be well to look at the things on display that stimulate our imagination and require careful scrutiny.

Eastern Airlines, the official airline of Walt Disneyworld, provides an illuminating picture of the spiritual search and the inner hungers of modern North Americans. I sit in the lounge waiting for the flight to be called. A flight from New York to Orlando (the home of Disneyworld) is a spiritual exercise requiring fortitude, courage, and imagination! It is spiritual because it both stretches the human spirit and also raises, in a poignant way, basic questions concerning human values and hopes. There is a look of expectancy and a deep longing in the eyes of my fellow passengers. There is an elderly couple returning to their retirement community, God's waiting room; there are the middle-aged using their children as an excuse to enter into fantasy: their pudgy overweight faces always moving, never still, chewing, smoking, laughing, anxious to be loved by their children. Then there's me and my clerical friend. He reads *How to Meditate* (bought at the airline bookstore, in the Occult section) while I muse on my fellow passengers and feel both cynical and guilty about my judgmentalism. Only the children still retain a breath of innocence and genuine expectation. They hold out to the jaundiced adults the promise of a lost joy, a mislaid integrity.

The passengers are noisy, expectant, pushy, and hungry for something. They are sheep without a shepherd. I feel humbled and ashamed: am I not as lost as they, needing the gracious love of the one shepherd? I share their longings and their fate. I too am faced with the inevitability of death. Spiritual direction? What direction? Where is everyone going? Who is doing the directing? There is no doubt that to me and to my companion (his attention has shifted to the children) that we all somehow are part of a pilgrimage, part of a movement to the sun and to the south. We are all on a journey. There is a sense of destiny at work here.

This familiar scene at a busy airport brought home to me forcefully the fact that we are all engaged, even now, in some form of spiritual direction. We are all going somewhere, but who or what is directing us is an open question. We all feel our hearts yearn for some terrific thing, but we're not sure what it is.

The spiritual supermarket tries to cater to our longings, fantasies, and hopes. It stimulates my appetite, but rarely satisfies my deepest hungers. I need companions who will help me find nutritious as opposed to junk food. What do I long for? For wholeness? For love? For healing? For the good life? For beautiful people? Surely yes! My desire is for the good and the beautiful, and this desire can be easily exploited. My immediate desires and short-term wants often get the better of me. St. Augustine reminds us over and over again that we are nothing else but a desire and a capacity for love. This loving capacity is a given. It is simply there. The task of spiritual guidance is to direct our hearts to love the only One who will ever satisfy us. We rightly desire what is good and what is beautiful, but our craving is such that we easily mistake a plastic replica for the real thing. There are plenty of practitioners in the art of human manipulation willing to sell us replicas of what is truly good and beautiful. Thus we are all engaged in spiritual direction in two senses. We are already seeking and receiving a sense of direction for our lives. We are on a journey, searching for direction and, at the same time, we are being directed or even propelled into the future. That is why it is important for us to be careful about the things we pay attention to because that which catches our attention tends to shape and guide our lives. I wonder, for example, how many of us are unconsciously guided by television. Soap operas provide many with moral and spiritual sustenance. They are like junk-food stopovers in lives busily going nowhere.

If we are to examine spiritual direction in the context of our actual desires and aspirations, we will have to look at the various ways in which society tries to meet them. How do we alleviate our sense of disappointment, our feeling of being let down when the goods we consume do not come through with what they promise? When the good and the beautiful turn out to be plastic and therefore fail to feed us? To whom can we turn in moments of disappointment and despair? Is it possible to tranquilize the restlessness of the human spirit with the promise that the good and the beautiful are just around the corner? And while we ache for that which is just around the corner life slips by us. We discover that one can miss one's life as one misses a plane.[1]

For Christians, the good and the beautiful are made concrete and personal in Jesus Christ, in a savior, not in a technique or program for self-improvement. Christianity is an invitation into a drama, a love story, and our sense of direction is given us in story form both in scripture and in the drama of the liturgy. My companions, too, are there to remind me of my part in the drama.

What are the characteristics of this love which comes to us in story form? What are the qualities that make it beautiful? In medieval theology there are three essential qualities in the concept of beauty and these same qualities give shape to healthy spiritual guidance. They are *integrity, harmony,* and *radiance.* A thing of beauty will have a unity, a wholeness, an integrity about it. It will harmonize discordant elements and make consonant the complexities. It will be clear, unequivocal, and radiant because it has but a single aim and purity of purpose. This is not the place to discuss questions of aesthetics. I simply want to suggest that this way of analyzing beauty might be applied usefully to ideas about mental and spiritual maturity, particularly in a supermarket age where beauty is often reduced to cosmetics. Integrity, harmony, and radiance are appropriate words to describe what it is to be a full human being. From an ordinary human point of view, they point to an ever-widening range of possibilities for us, and form a specifically Christian viewpoint, they describe the healing and hope that Christ brings to the whole human family. Christ invites us to participate in his crucified, risen, and ascended life as the means by which we are given integrity, harmony, and radiance. In short, to be in Christ is to be truly beautiful.

These three words can also be used to join the therapeutic and the spiritual, to heal the breach that exists in some people's minds between psychology and religion. If it is seen and believed that it is the Holy Spirit himself who is the director, that it is he who undergirds human life, growth, and potential, then two things happen: psychology is put in its place (vital but subordinate) and the Holy Spirit is accepted as the real initiator and creator of human life and community. We need to be rescued from the damaging reductionist tendency that wishes to explain everything in psychological terms. The psychologism has infected the Church and, in particular, the important field of pastoral counseling. Why is it that many who are trained in the area of pastoral counseling are abysmally ignorant of the tradition of spiritual direction? Why is it that many who are interested in the life of the Spirit are repelled by or ignorant of depth psychology? I think it is time to effect a coming together.

Three things have happened to me personally to encourage me to see the possibilities for a marriage between the best of the insights of depth psychology and those of the Christian spiritual tradition.

The first happened some years ago when I tried to write a paper to show a clear and unequivocal demarcation line between therapy and spiritual direction. I had served on our diocesan committee for professional development and had become tired and irritated in our having to dole out money to enable priests to flee into counseling: I failed miserably in my task to separate the psychological from the spiritual. Instead, I began to realize the enormous area of overlap between therapy and spiritual direction in the common concern for integrity, harmony, and radiance.

The second event came a little later on when a distinguished career priest came to see me about and for spiritual direction. He was rector of a large and prestigious parish. He ran a thriving counseling center, having modeled it and the parish on the best insights of organizational development. His own personal life had suffered in the meantime, and he had grown to a new awareness of his own deep spiritual needs. He suggested the need for places where people could come for specific spiritual direction as well as for pastoral counseling, and he outlined a plan for establishing such a center in his own parish which would be run separate from, but in conjunction with, the work in pastoral counseling. I was invited to the parish, met the counselors, and from this encounter I have gained a new appreciation of the need we have to integrate our pastoral counseling with spiritual direction; or, to put it in a more polemical way, we need to make sure that our pastoral counseling is theologically grounded. This is not to say that those who are engaged in counseling in a Christian context are not also engaged in some form of spiritual direction. It is just that what is implicit here needs to be made explicit. There are marvelous treasures to be shared on both sides and we need to be more aware of them.

The third event is the most important and most difficult to describe. It involves a relationship begun several years ago with a woman (over seventy) who was steeped in the literature and devotion of the Catholic tradition. She is a member of an Anglican religious community that has been through several experiences of upheaval in the "renewal" that occurred after the Second Vatican Council. She was deeply influenced by the mystical tradition and yet was able to acknowledge gratefully the insights of depth psychology. During our time together there were many tears, many sessions involving healing and mutual spiritual direction. Some

time ago she sent me a letter that combines in one person's experience the unity of the therapeutic and the redemptive, the longing
we all share for integrity, harmony, and radiance. She sent me for
my birthday a postcard of the icon of the Baptism of Christ. In it
is expressed the rich symbolism of the Eastern Church, including
the water demons who are crushed by the descent of Christ into the
waters. This is what she wrote:

> It is a real icon, now, the point of meeting between my now and
> God's eternity, and was the entrance into an experience which
> was an inversion of the strange gloomy Sunday just before Ash
> Wednesday last year, when I had such an overwhelming sense
> of *convergence*, that I could not eat and walked instead, for
> hours, in the street, warm as toast . . . It was an experience of
> going down into the cold depths, where the water spirits are, and
> taking my "little girl," my angry, shameful, resentful, lazy, treach-
> erous little girl, with me in much love, down where the "unoffend-
> ing feet" still shine, and then, together, the little girl and I, who
> are one, and the Lord prayed for those who have brought me to
> that dark cold place. It was a moment of reconciliation, and
> whether or not I can express it or hear anyone reply, it is a place
> I can return to, and a permanent radical attitude below the
> surface scuffles. Pray that the Holy Spirit will keep my roots
> there, and in forgiving love.

The key word is perhaps convergence, the coming together of
many ideas and many levels of consciousness *in the Lord*. It is the
acceptance of the creative presence of Christ in even our darkest
place that is so strongly emphasized in spiritual direction. It is this
naked confidence in God's love which makes us dare to enter the
battle. Spiritual direction is concerned with the deeper knowledge
that it is the Holy Spirit who is sanctifier and healer. This is at the
heart of Christian spirituality. It is never primarily a technique. It
is a gift. There is no way, in the intimacy of the Spirit, that we can
pose as experts and lord it over one another. Once we have understood this much we can move through the spiritual supermarket
with a critical and competent eye.

Let us take a fresh look at the psychoanalytic model. Psychiatry
needs to be demythologized, not in order to debunk, but merely to
dethrone. Some, in repressing their vocation to be spiritual guides,
have been intimidated by the expertise of the medical and thera-

peutic professions. Psychiatry at its worst is in a state of confusion and disarray; at best, in a period of ferment and stocktaking. The various theories, techniques, and methods vie for our attention. The signals one receives from the psychiatric profession are themselves ambiguous. "Psychiatry has come of age," "Psychiatry is dying." Perhaps mental illness is a myth we have invented? The schizophrenic may be a lot "saner" than we are. Such disarray need not dismay us (nor give us reason to rejoice). This critical state of affairs demonstrates that integrity, harmony, and radiance are costly and exist not in a consumers' paradise, but in a community whose highest value is love freely given. Our psychological confusions make the point clear that mental and spiritual health is really a theological issue, that is, it is about God. Spiritual direction is rooted in a specific understanding of what a human being is; it is grounded in what we might call the Christology of humanity. Who am I? I am, by definition, one who is loved by Christ. This constitutes my humanity. To be fully human is to live in the Spirit, to be inhabited by God in mutual fellowship.

It is not psychotherapy's fault that it has become a surrogate religion. It is largely ours. We tend to lay upon it an enormously heavy burden. We say to the therapist, "My world is broken and you've got to fix it." Psychotherapists are forced to deal with the basic religious question of meaning, and this is fundamentally a question about what a human being finally is. Unless that question is resolved in some way all our discipline and striving are to no purpose. John Updike, in his novel *The Coup*, describes an American woman who had never considered the fundamental question of what a human being is. She is the rejected wife of a black Muslim Marxist dictator of an emerging African nation. This is the way Updike describes her:

> Her clinical epithets reminded me of her book-club books—the warping, fading, termite-riddled stacks and rows of volumes imported from her native land, popular psychology and sociology mostly. How to succeed, how to be saved, how to survive a mid-life crisis, how to find fulfillment within feminity, how to be free, how to love, how to face death, how to harness your fantasies, how to make dollars in your spare time—the endless self-help and self-exploration of a performance-oriented race that has

never settled within itself the fundamental question of what a
man is. A man is a clot of blood. Hopeful books, they disinte-
grated rapidly in this climate; she had run out of shelf space and
stacked this literary foreign aid on the floor, where our great
sub-continent of insects hollowed out the covers from underneath, their invisible chewing a re-run of the chewing of her eyes
as she read away the monotonous succession of her days, weeks,
and years.[2]

We begin as a clot of blood, but a clot of blood on whom God has
indelibly marked his eternal love. No wonder we need help and
guidance in finding a balance between our humble origins and our
divine destiny.

Of all the many schools of psychotherapy, transpersonal therapy
is the one that has the most in common with spiritual direction. This
school is frankly religious in orientation and is therefore most
appealing (and hence most dangerous). This form of therapy includes the cosmos on its agenda. It tries to be all-inclusive and, as
such, is a potential ally and rival of Christian spirituality. This
school includes Arica Training, Transcendental Meditation, and
Psychosynthesis.

What are we to make of all this? Whether we like it or not, we
are in the midst of an upheaval of consciousness that is affecting us
all. In a sense we have no choice but to be affected by this upheaval.
We absorb the atmosphere in the culture as surely as we breathe
the air around us. One psychiatrist writes:

> The evolution of human awareness is not a smooth, steady contin-
> uum. Rather, it proceeds in sudden discontinuous steps, in which
> each move to a higher place of awareness is achieved by revela-
> tion, by a new view of the human individual in his wholeness.
> Freud's articulation of the basic concepts of psychoanalysis is one
> of those revelatory steps in the evolution of consciousness. That
> revelation, to put it simply, provided us with the following con-
> cepts: the dynamic unconscious (our actions are determined by
> unknown forces), transference (we unwittingly carry attitudes
> born in old relationships into the new), and consciousness as cure
> (once we are made aware of what troubles us, it loses its hold on
> us). These concepts represent a real advance in our grasp of
> human possibilities,[3]

and (I would add) can help to deepen and nurture our understanding of the gospel.

What is significant here in the comments of this psychiatrist is his use of the strange words *revelation* and *revelatory*. Revelation is the new breaking in and (as in Christ) reconstructing reality. It is a transcendent event in the light of which one's perception of reality changes. It sounds strangely like the dynamics of what we call conversion, and the Freudian concepts, in this context, are compatible with the traditional understanding of spiritual direction as concerned with the dynamic unconscious, transference, and heightened consciousness.

We are living at a new level of awareness. This does not make us better than our ancestors, but it does mean that "there is no return to our lost innocence." The concepts of psychoanalysis, often half-digested or even caricatured, have now, whether we like it or not, become part of the very fabric of the way in which we view and interpret reality. While I am making no special claims for psychotherapy, I do suggest that we have suffered from a form of spirituality that has repressed the awful knowledge which the psychoanalytic revolution has brought us. The age of innocence is over. Freud and Jung have carefully documented the Fall of Adam and Eve, but have also given us new insights concerning the meaning of grace and redemption. The doctrine of justification by faith alone, for example, has taken on a healing dynamism for me. The more I know about the workings of my labyrinthine psyche, the more I am convinced of my need for a savior! And my need for the Savior brings me into a fellowship of pilgrims who offer companionship along the way.

As it has matured, the psychotherapeutic profession, in the context of our longing for companionship, has been forced to ask fundamental religious questions concerning meaning and death, and many psychotherapists are beginning to see their role as a guru with spiritual as well as psychological insight. There is a genuine coming together of persons from the various helping professions, who are now finding themselves defining common goals and realizing that they are in the realm of the mystery in the kingdom of the Spirit.

Sheldon Kopp is one such guru-therapist.[4] His own inner life was revolutionized by his having to face the terror of death in a serious illness, and from that revelatory experience he ceased being a mere practitioner and became a pilgrim, now seeing his role as a therapist in the light of our common pilgrimage. Kopp's description of the therapist could well be applied to our understanding of the spiritual director. "The therapist . . . provides another struggling human being to be encountered by the then self-centered patient who can see no other problems than his own.[5] Kopp describes seven marks of the guru-therapist:

1. He is another struggling human being.
2. He can interpret the other to himself by virtue of his not being the patient. (But the healing process requires us to be thoroughly committed to our own being in the encounter with others and not to a *role* as therapist or spiritual director.)
3. He can advise.
4. He can provide emotional acceptance and support that nurtures personal growth.
5. Above all, he can listen: He "will *listen* actively and purposefully, responding with the instrument of his trade, that is, with the personal vulnerability of his own trembling self."
6. This listening will facilitate the patient's telling his tale, the telling that can set him free.
7. Lastly, images and symbols on which one can meditate, and through which one might discover one's identity, rise up through the encounter.

This last point cannot be overemphasized. We live in our images, by our symbols. They are the mortar that holds reality together for us. That is why such issues as the revision of the liturgy and the roles of the sexes stir up the deepest parts of the psyche. They touch our lives at the symbolic level. They work a change of metaphor, a symbol, of imagery, and it is by such things that we human beings live. As we shall see in a later chapter, the spiritual director must be a person who can live on various levels with varying sets of metaphors and images if he is to listen sympathetically, if his heart is to be genuinely open to those who come for spiritual guidance. It requires the peculiar grace of being able to live simultaneously in different worlds: in the realm of the psychotherapeutic, and in the dimension of the spiritual. Both worlds are united in the spiritual, for the greater (the spiritual) contains the lesser (the therapeutic).

The therapists who acknowledge this fundamental spiritual structure of reality see themselves as persons on pilgrimage, persons of the spirit. The therapist may, writes Kopp,

> Only get to keep that which he is willing to let go of. The cool water of the running stream may be scooped up with open, out-flowing palms. It cannot be grasped up to the mouth with clenched fists, no matter what thirst motivates our desperate grab.[6]

Some of us are called to be professional pilgrims, willing to guide others through the labyrinthine alleys of the supermarket, past the check-out counter and into another world to begin the life-giving and challenging journey into mystery. With us who are consciously responding to a call to be a companion, the medium is the message. We cannot convincingly *talk* about companionship without *being* a companion. We are a word about the Word. We are not to offer dogma. We are to offer ourselves. And this involves the cultivation of a naked awareness of and an all-daring confidence in God which enables us to trust him and not ourselves. "Doing therapy is like remembering all the time that you are really going to die. . . . Too often I forget that I am dying, that we each suffer from the same terminal disease. At such times, when I do not remember to remember, I blow it."[7]

This sounds very much like spiritual guidance. The way the patient views the therapist carries with it the same dangers as the way the penitent views the confessor or the person seeking guidance views the director.

> To this image they impute characteristics that not only do I not possess, but to which I do not even aspire. Often, for a time, I am seen by the patient as beyond anxiety, without conflicts, free of weaknesses, never foolish, incapable of evil, and always happy.
>
> I experience this idolization as a terrible burden. . . . Because I know that we are both unredeemed sinners, both wandering in exile, each equally vulnerable, I will not accept the burdensome illusion that we are not the same.[8]

Kopp knows little of the Christian tradition—where the crucial difference is that we are redeemed sinners—but he does know a great deal of the complexities of relationship of a guide to the wounded and lost.

The common longing that binds spiritual direction and therapy together is the restoration of a lost beauty. I do not mean beauty in any shallow and cosmetic sense. Redemption can be seen as the healing restoration of that divine beauty which was meant to be ours from the beginning and is therefore the work of Christ. William Johnston writes:

> Healing is progress and resurrection. It can best be understood by looking at the wounds of the risen Christ. These are still present. The resurrection did not take them away. But they are glorified, transfigured. Now they are beautiful.[9]

Healing, as the restoration of a lost beauty, a lost integrity, a lost harmony, a lost radiance can only be accomplished through love, and love depends on both adoration and commitment: adoration, which is simply loving attentiveness to God, and commitment, which is the willingness to obey the focus of our deepest attention. This means living consciously within the realm of the Holy Spirit. There is an undeniable sacredness in any healing relationship. Good therapists are able to show compassion without possession or attachment. One therapist writes, "The temptations are there. You get very sexy people, rich people, famous people. I have to set all those qualities aside so I can respond to them. Our relationship is a priestly one. . . ."[10]

The therapeutic pattern is a priestly one and it takes on the form of priesthood which is open to all human beings. The quarrel, then, is not with psychology or psychiatry, but with their reductionist practitioners. Buber criticized Jung for neglecting the supernatural grounds of spiritual experience. The stark and wonderful reality of God is the ground and source of all that is. Jung himself may not have forgotten this truth but many in the therapeutic professions and even some clergy have forgotten it.

There are, then, supernatural grounds for our desire to regain our integrity, to find harmony, to be radiant with life. We long to be beautiful, and this desire is planted in the human heart by God, the

Blessed Trinity who is the pattern of harmonious unity, of radiance shining through a communion of persons. The pilgrims of Disneyworld bear witness to this, and the hungry sheep look up to be fed. They crowd the supermarkets. Where do we stand in all this hunger, this need, this desire? I stand in the need of companionship. I need to learn what it is to do something beautiful for God.

For both therapist and director, insofar as each is participating in a double process of healing and of growth, love is the supreme requirement. Healing and growth can be impeded if the therapist or the director knows little of himself, of who he is and where he is going. In many ways the therapist and the spiritual director have a common goal. Therapy needs to be understood as something that is not just for the mentally ill, but also for those who want to grow as human beings. If we understand therapy in this way, then it becomes an ally instead of an enemy to spiritual guidance.

There are, then, many similarities between psychotherapy and spiritual direction and it would be a poor spiritual director who did not have at least an intuitive knowledge of his psychological self and was unable to use some of the insights of psychotherapy in spiritual direction. The difference between the two is found not so much in practice but in faith orientation. The spiritual director is, by definition, Christ-centered, and spiritual direction is an act of worship because both the director and the directee understand themselves to be in the presence of God. The psychotherapist can believe this, too, but it is not necessary. Where the two work together is in a common commitment to help the people who come to them be as free as possible from illusions about themselves and the world in which they live. There is an innate tendency in all of us to want to control and manipulate reality in order to feel secure. We do this by distorting our inner world by presenting to the outside a self that is untrue; a mask. We also manipulate and organize the external world to reinforce our feelings of security by treating other people as objects. Psychotherapy understands, well enough, the metaphor of battle when it comes to our longing for a safe place.

The battle is often fought around the issues of security. Our longing for it is so deep that we will cling to anything that promises it; to religion, to philosophy, to political ideology. The hard thing is to face the fact that faith requires us to trust the unknown future not because it is safe (in a shallow form of our own making), but because it is God's!

Faith helps erode the supermarket mentality that infects us, particularly in the affluent West. I am often overstimulated by ideas and thoughts. I need to get out of the supermarket, where I *choose* what I want to buy, and learn in faith what it means to *be chosen*. Both therapy and spiritual direction, in their different ways, can help me get out of my consumer mind-set. Spiritual companionship helps me move from being a consumer to being a lover and a friend.

Before we proceed, let us ask ourselves three simple questions:

1. Do I really believe that my life comes to me as a gift and that there is in me a terrific thing?

2. Am I, in the middle of my own struggles, daring enough to ask for help, seek guidance, cultivate friendships?

3. Am I sincere in wanting to respond to my longing for God, especially when I know and fear the revolutionary changes that may be involved?

3

Upheaval and Change
The Alliance Between Therapy and Spirituality

Am I sincere in wanting to respond to my longing for God especially when I know and fear the revolutionary changes which may be involved?

A t the end of the last chapter three questions were asked concerning the giftedness of life, the necessity for guidance, and the inevitability of upheaval and change. These are three ingredients always present in genuine human companionship. In this and the next two chapters we will be concerned with these three issues. Let us look at the last question first.

We live in a wild time: a time of excitement and ambiguity, a time of wonder and upheaval. Our culture is characterized by manic-depressive tendencies with regard to both its interior and exterior lives. There is wild enthusiasm, great excitement, and expectancy in the air and our lives tend to fluctuate between despair and hope. Everything holds out the double promise of life and death. The human race is facing what seems to be insuperable problems: overpopulation, the exhaustion and pollution of natural resources, a critical change of life style, and even the threat of annihilation in a nuclear holocaust. At such times there is a passion for religious and political security. The last thing I want when everything is falling apart is to change.

In our larger cities there is evidence of a not-so-quiet desperation which erupts violently and irrationally in the lives of apparently well-put-together people. But the prospect isn't all bad. The trouble is that we cannot always tell which upheavals in our lives are death-dealing and which are life-bearing. We have to live with an enormous amount of insecurity whether we like it or not. Many "unknowns" threaten us. The upheavals and changes are sometimes insidious because we cannot always tell that they are happening. It is amazing how we go on with "business as usual" even in the worst of times. When I was a child, tea was always served at 4:00 P.M. It was served with utter regularity no matter what was happening elsewhere. I suspect that tea will be served at that civilized hour not only at the Last Judgment, but also in heaven itself! This passion for order and regularity is not to be despised, but taken to extremes it can blind us to the upheavals and changes going on around us. Or worse, we can *appear* to have adapted to new circumstances, but underneath keep everything the same. On the other hand, change and upheaval for their own sake have no value; Kierkegaard speaks of the kind of revolution which "leaves everything standing but cunningly empties it of its significance."

When we accept our need for help and our capacity for giving help to others, we cannot but acknowledge the challenges and opportunities ahead. As we explore the importance of a revival of spiritual guidance, we need to take warning. I say to myself, "Beware of those who would guide you. But even more, beware of those tendencies within you that yearn for easy answers, superficial security, and sentimental vision." We are all peculiarly vulnerable to manipulation today, for we live in an era when our lostness and loneliness can be brutally exploited. While there are glorious opportunities for personal and communal growth in the Spirit, so also are there deep and pervasive spiritual and psychological tyrannies.

There can be, therefore, serious problems with the language we use to describe guidance of any kind. The title "spiritual director" can suggest a form of tyranny. One member of a religious community said to me once that the direction she received in her novitiate could be summed up in two frightful words: "Destroy Yourself!" Here was a terrible confusion between a path of self-destruction and one of self-surrender. Sometimes these two paths look alike and a spiritual guide can help us tell the crucial difference. One path leads to life, the other to death. Some forms of spirituality feed people's destructive tendencies. For example, the kind of spirituality that tends to despise the body and the energy of the passions leads to a form of guidance where people are unhappy about their bodies and are fearful of their deepest impulses. No wonder that upheaval and change are thought of as things to be avoided.

Even where direction is open and healthy and where upheaval and change are seen as potentially creative, there is the danger of our developing one-sided relationships. Mutuality and reciprocity are lost when, for example, one person in a relationship is seen as the needy partner, while the other is the one able to meet the needs. We set up fences between doctor and patient, between the sick and the healthy, between the enlightened and the dullard. Christian companionship is committed to tearing down such fences. They may be important for some kinds of relationships, but such class distinction is inimical to true spiritual friendship. Thus even with a less jaundiced view of things, the very word *direction* brings to mind a one-sided relationship and the ever-present possibility of unhealthy submission.

My longing for companionship often betrays a need in me to hide inside a shallow intimacy which costs nothing. I am tempted to overcome my feeling of separateness by cheap tricks which produce the illusion of warmth and community. When I realize the cost of true companionship, I shrink back. It would, for example, be a strong person who could resist a shallow interpretation of Transactional Analysis, and be willing to pay the high personal price which self-knowledge always entails. To get to the point of being able to say: "I'm O.K. You're O.K." (which characterizes T.A. at its best) is extremely costly. No matter which way we approach this, companionship is always expensive.

Modern psychology has done much to aid us in both the knowledge of God and the knowledge of self. I do not mean to imply that we really know more spiritually than our ancestors. We do, however, apprehend things in a different way. We have a different style of knowing which is better suited to our survival in the second half of the twentieth century. Modern psychology has enabled us to cope better with who we are. This is in no way to suggest that our ancestors were our moral, intellectual, and spiritual inferiors. The psychologist has made us realize that we not only possess the passionate desire *to know* (all the great philosophers since Plato knew that), we also carry within us the equally strong passion *to be known.*

> As one critic has written: "With the psychologists we felt finally known. But as time has shown, not deeply known. Therein lies the disillusionment with modern psychology. The scale was too small against which we measured our failures as man. So that all the self-acceptance in the world (which was the mercy of modern psychology) could not help us but kept us mired in illusions about ourselves. In attempting to free us from neurotic guilt, psychology only helped us for a time to feel comfortable about ourselves, but never to discover the struggle for greater being. The reason was that the method of self-acceptance was too small, too egoistic and introverted."[1]

We ached for self-acceptance, and it is often a friend accepting us as we are which enables us to begin to accept ourselves. But the acceptance has to be genuine. I want the deepest part of me to be accepted, not my sanitized, plastic, cosmetic self.

Only in companionship with fellow pilgrims can I begin to tell the difference between that in me which is more me than myself and that in me which is wearing the mask or the make-up of an assigned role. Without you as companion and friend I confuse the outer shell with the inner substance. That is why I sometimes get angry and frustrated with people who say, "Relax, and be yourself!" I know they mean well by this command, but it only serves to aggravate the problem. Only by the nurturing and probing of companions can the deeper self emerge. I remember being given a button to wear at a conference some years ago. It had one word on it: "BE!" and while I longed to BE with a capital *B*, I pointed out that I need Christian companionship, worship, and nurture in order to discover what it might mean to BE. On that particular day for me to BE would have meant letting a great deal of sourness and mean-spiritedness spill out. Maybe that was what was expected. The point is that psychology has taught me that I have many selves, that there is a whole cast of characters in me who would like to BE. The Christian faith, on the other hand, assures me that in the fellowship of Christ I can trust that the deepest in me, behind the list of actors, is one whom God knows and loves.

The value of modern psychology is that it leaves us with the hope that we can really grow and change. What psychology does not do is to help us choose the direction that growth and change should take. How do we tell the true from the false in matters of the Spirit? There's the problem. Psychology shows that psychology is not enough, that it is only a means and not an end. A psychiatrist friend of mine says that all he can do psychologically is to help mend a few broken bones so that a person can continue his or her journey. He can get them moving, but he cannot tell them which road to take. For us to choose the direction of growth and change (especially when, on one level, the end of it all is death), there has to be faith. Our problem, therefore, is not one of technique, whether it be with regard to the diseases of the soul or to world hunger. We have the expertise and techniques at our fingertips. The issue is not technique, but faith. And faith that is a commitment to a particular Way is the means by which we tell the true from the false in the direction our life is to take. That is why the therapists with whom I increasingly come into contact are asking spiritual (that is, faith) questions.

For me, the Way is Christ, and my being able to tell the true from the false in my life is dependent on my walking the Christian Way. Thus for Christians, the supreme means by which we know and are known is bound up with "keeping in touch with Jesus." The object of spiritual direction is to help us keep in touch with Jesus as the key to true companionship, the bearer of meaning and value, and the power over sin and death. Spiritual direction seeks to guide us deeper into the double mystery of God and of ourselves by means of companionship. That mystery opens up when we read the Bible and when we break the bread in the Eucharist. It also opens up as we learn to touch one another as ends and not means, as walking mysteries, images of God.

Direction of one sort or another is vital when we begin to understand that our Christian commitment is a journey, a pilgrimage, a quest. We need to receive and to give support to one another on what can often be a rough road. In religious matters there is a double need for direction. First, there is, as we have seen, the need to be able to tell the difference between the real and the unreal. Direction can help us tell which is which. The second need is in the pursuit of the real once it has been apprehended. Jesus, in the Fourth Gospel, is described as the one who meets the double need. As the Way, the Truth, and the Life, Jesus helps us tell the difference between the real and the unreal. He also invites us to commit ourselves to the Real.

Talking about the Real is as difficult as talking about being. Talk is not enough. We want someone to show us in his person what it means to be real. Jesus does just that for those who have faith. A biblical word that comes close to the words *reality* and *being* is *glory*. Glory means "being in all its fullness," and we are on a pilgrimage from glory to glory. We are on a journey from what is less real to what is more real; we need all the help we can get in continually testing for reality. We need a touchstone, we need criteria. Our touchstone is Jesus. Our criteria are bound up with his death and resurrection understood as events that have power to free us now.

One way of distinguishing spiritual direction from therapy is the acknowledged faith commitment of both parties in an atmosphere of reverence and awe. Spiritual direction is an act of worship. There are certain things that Christian obedience requires which place spiritual direction in a markedly different context from that of therapy. The world view of the Christian is characterized by repentance and conversion. We Christians are called upon to cultivate a turning to the Lord. For us to be bearers of good news we must also know from within what it is to be forgiven, what it is, in some sense, to be raised from the dead. Salvation is the deepest form of therapy we can ever know, and Christ has often been understood as therapist in the literal sense of the word: physician. The cross is the medicine that will heal the world. T. S. Eliot called Christ the wounded surgeon whose sensitive blade probes and questions the distempered part.

Both therapy and spirituality wish to deal with the whole person and not with bits and pieces. I, for example, tend to discuss ordinary things first in spiritual direction. "When did you last go to a movie, read a book, have fun? Are you eating properly? Do you get enough sleep?" All these things point to the context of the spiritual life and need to be discussed before we can explore together the creative dimensions of contemplative prayer. In other words, I find myself asking questions concerning the ordinary shape of a person's life. On the other hand, therapist friends of mine not only ask the ordinary questions, but also find themselves being asked questions which properly belong to the dimension of faith. A good therapist, for example, can be a great aid to a person's spiritual growth in prayer.

Prayer, like breathing, needs a free environment. Enormous weights on the chest are not conducive to easy breathing and there are many psychological weights which press down upon the soul and inhibit its relationship with God. Prayer is not so much a duty as a natural function, and it has been my colleagues in the counseling and psychiatric disciplines that have helped me to see just that.

There has, therefore, been, in my own experience, a happy alliance between two great traditions—between the therapeutic and the spiritual. The effect of this alliance has yet to be felt in all quarters. Many in the Church are still fearful or suspicious about anything to do with psychology, and this uneasiness is often to be found among those who might value the insights of psychology the most—among, for example, those who emphasize the importance of direct personal experience in religions. They would find in psychology an ally with regard to the interpretation and evaluation of any claim a person may have to have encountered God.

At the heart of the Christian religion is the claim that God dwells with his people. He is Immanuel—God-with-us—and our age is characterized by its longing for direct personal experience of this God. There is glory and danger ahead in the life of the churches and the signs are ambiguous. We are undergoing an exhilarating if confusing revival of life in the spirit. The Charismatic Movement (that umbrella term to cover a multitude of experiences) is a double-headed monster. A charismatic person can be one who radiates the love of God in the power of the Holy Spirit. On the other hand, he or she can display a destructive arrogance that could give rise to a mindless fanaticism. There is no human being more joyous than one who has been touched by the power of the Holy Spirit. At the same time, there is no more frightening and pathetic phenomenon than a human being who *imagines* that what possesses him is the Holy Spirit. Combine so-called "charismatic" experience with mental imbalance and there is literally hell to pay. The issue of discernment is, therefore, one of the most pressing for today's world, and the insights of psychology can help us sort out the true from the false.

We have to face such questions as: How do we know when the Holy Spirit is at work? How can we discern the will of God for us now? How can I get to what I really want? How do I get out of that double bind? What I want the most is often what I avoid the most. How can I get to the place where I really want to be? Where can I find a trustworthy guide or friend to counsel me? What do I really believe? Is there a power to change and save us?

After all these warnings and questions, I want to affirm the belief in a power that is not only within us, but also above and beyond us. That power is the Holy Spirit of God. A spiritual director, therefore, is never merely a director of conscience. He or she is above all charismatic, that is, he or she works within the realm of the Spirit. Our object is not to bring to birth our own spiritual children and thereby foster a father/son, mother/daughter, parent/child, master/pupil relationship. No! The child is God's already. Although one metaphor for the spiritual director is that of midwife, we need other images that will illuminate the task of the spiritual director after the work of the midwife is over. There is the need for mutual companionship after the spiritual rebirth. We can assist one another in the many adventures of the spirit once the journey has begun. Human beings can, in the power of the Spirit, change and be rescued from the various slaveries and tyrannies to which they have been subject. There is, mediated through the Church, a personal and sacramental power which can free us to be, to grow, to become. That same Spirit is working in us right now. Sometimes it is difficult to believe this. There are moments when I either do not believe in this transfiguring power or am fearful of it. It is easier to opt for a shallow therapy, which offers band-aid sort of counseling rather than the deep healing of radical redemption. It is at such times that I ask myself the question: Am I sincere in wanting to respond to my longing for God, especially when I know and fear the revolutionary changes that may be involved?

One way of avoiding such inner revolution is, paradoxically, to become an expert. Those who enter the therapeutic professions are known to be motivated in part by their own needs, hungers, and fears. In a similar fashion, the ordained ministry can become a haven for those avoiding the inner upheaval which commitment to Christ involves. One psychotherapist writes:

> I remember one tortured young clergyman whose underlying motivation for seeking help was the growing recognition that he had learned the tricks of successful ministry in the absence of really feelingful spiritual substance. The superficial manipulative skills, which had served to make him appealing to many, were growing ineffective as he began to realize that his brand of inspirational goodness was a subtle form of evil, that he was up to no good. The week of his first meeting with me, he had dreamed that he was a powerful warlock casting spells. But in his dream he found all at once that his magical gestures and incantations no longer forked any lightning. He hexed impotently with his hands and muttered sorcerer's gibberish only to discover that for the first time no one was controlled by his witchcraft. That was the beginning of a long struggle which gradually allowed him to reclaim and renew his faith, not through control of others but through surrender to himself."[2]

The way through is to give up the need for control and to surrender to the deepest longings in us. These are difficult things to do, especially for experts.

We can escape from upheaval and change in two ways. First, we can move into a safe but arid intellectualism. This is the temptation of theologians. Or we can become a sort of spiritual lepidopterist, collecting inner experiences by which to work our magic on others. Two chance remarks made me realize how easy it is for religious people to avoid the very thing they claim they are seeking. The first was a remark made by a Japanese bishop with regard to the impact an English monk, Father Herbert Kelly, made on Japanese clergy during the first part of this century: "Under Father Kelly's influence some of them ceased to be slaves to theology and became free men in Christ." The second remark was made in exasperation by a priest about a woman who collected spiritual experiences: "The trouble with her is that she knows all of the words and none of the music!" Without the help of companions, I easily fall into the trap of intellectualism on the one hand or that of experience on the other. This is not to deny the importance of either. It is simply to point out that companionship is essential if I am to keep on the right path.

What better way for me to avoid the radical commitment de-
manded of me than to become a spiritual guide? I am sure this was
one of the many motives behind my wanting to teach the subject!
Perhaps it wasn't such a bad thing after all, because in teaching it
I have been slowly brought to the realization that I am being
formed by the Christian tradition. I am truly in the hands of my
companions.

It is natural that we who will respond to the call to be a companion to others want to be as skilled and prepared as possible. There
is, after all, no virtue in incompetence. The simple truth is that the
guide needs guidance too. Unless he or she is, in one way or other,
responsible to another, then it is easy to use the relationship in
spiritual direction not only to control and manipulate another person, but also to avoid the painful growth that is required of both
the director and directee alike. The task sounds noble enough: to
alleviate pain and to foster growth. It is quite another matter to be
willing to walk with people into their hurt, to help them penetrate
the dark places within themselves. The director is called to be a true
companion by exposing himself to the same dangers and opportunities as his fellow pilgrim.

In the realm of spiritual and psychic health there are no experts,
only fellow pilgrims. The therapist and the director of souls are ones
who have first diagnosed their own sickness. They are wounded
healers. Our struggles, disappointments, and restlessness can be
signs of hope seeking space in the human heart. The struggles are
a sign that we are unfinished and incomplete animals. There is hope
in knowing that a human being is a movement towards God, and
that this movement leads us into worship, faith, and surrender.

How can I respond sincerely to my longing for God without
worship becoming central to my life? And true worship requires
the loss of self, the saying of a wholehearted Yes to God. I have to
be the slave of some god or other. That much is clear. The question
is which god? Simone Weil knew that surrender was essential. Once
she watched the blessing of the Portuguese fishing fleet, with the
wives of the fishermen going from ship to ship carrying candles and
singing ancient songs. For her it was a moment of great illumina-
tion and she concluded: "Christianity is preeminently the religion
of slaves, that slaves cannot help belonging to it and I among
them."[3] We are slaves of a god. Which one?

We believe that there is One whose service is perfect freedom. Thus, for Christians the answer is clear: Christians are those who have surrendered to God in Christ and the Spirit calls us into companionship with one another. It is all a question of surrender, of self-abandonment, and we need the fellowship of our fellow pilgrims to do this in a creative way. We cannot help but tremble on the brink of surrender, but it is our companions who give us the courage to jump. It is at such moments of surrender that we become truly ecstatic. Christian ecstasy causes us to go beyond ourselves and to stand outside the narrow view we have of our selves. It is then that the Holy Spirit gives us back a self loved, broadened, and deepened by the loss of self.

All this activity needs a context in which to flourish. Even though much appears to be happening inside me, it is not my work. I am part of something bigger than myself, and unless I see myself as part of a living and flowing river, buoyed up by the care and nurture of others, I will find myself drowning, dragged under by my own willful self-sufficiency. I need the fellowship of the Church which will allow me to make mistakes and ask questions.

The gospel puts an enormous question mark beside all standards of spiritual and mental health insofar as they would narrowly circumscribe the self. When certain kinds of mental and spiritual disorder are "cured," the clumsy surgeon will tear out creative along with destructive elements. Indeed there is often a place for the apparently destructive and erroneous in us. It is simply a question of misplaced energy. It is what St. Augustine would call the energy of love, of disordered love, but still love. The poet Goethe, in his work *Wilhelm Meister*, wrote:

> Not to keep men from error is the duty of the educator of men, but to guide the erring one, even to let him swill his error out of full cups—that is the wisdom of teachers.[4]

This truth, above all others, disturbs me the most about this art of arts and makes me fearful and want to draw back. How often in giving spiritual direction do I sense that what disturbs and destroys in the soul is inextricably bound up with a creative and overflowing energy! How often does the so-called aberration of my fellow pilgrim throw light on the malaise of my own soul! How often in counseling, confession, conversation with a soul friend, am I overcome with the unnerving good news that I am what my brother is, what my sister is. If they are disturbed, upset, sick, then so am I. If they are overjoyed and full of wonder, then so am I. The more I am allowed the privilege of entering another person, entering into his or her individuality and uniqueness, the more am I overcome with a sense of our common destiny. We are truly companions. There is no well-defined relationship of the expert to the inept. I may have certain skills, which may be helpful to another, but in the experience of spiritual direction itself I am ministered to by the one who seeks my help.

I am often shocked into the realization that, as a priest, confessor, and friend, I may have to help others go deeper into pain and darkness, and that if this happens, I must stay with them. The temptation for the therapist and spiritual director alike is to throw a pallid superficial light on pain that is often far too deep for technique and skills, but not too deep for the Spirit. It is in this deeper realm where the spiritual director and therapist begin to discard their professional masks and become true spiritual guides. As a spiritual director, I know I need the expertise, the diagnostic skill of the psychotherapist; the psychotherapist also needs something that the spiritual director has to offer: the dimension of worship, adoration, and mystery in the face of the Other who is God and of the other who is his fellow human being.

What then is the proper context of spiritual direction as opposed to therapy? Prayer, adoration, liturgy, worship—all in the conscious acknowledgment of the presence and power of the Holy Spirit: that is the context of spiritual direction. Under the aegis of the Spirit, anything can happen! There is from the outset an explicit realization simply that GOD IS! Problems of belief, of prayer, of worship, of meaning and death are opened up within this context. The director needs to know the signs of psychological sickness, and, if necessary, refer the person to a therapist competent to deal with these things. It is only when a person has a certain amount of self-knowledge that he or she is ready for *spiritual* direction. The person utterly occupied with himself is not ready for the mutuality of Christian companionship. There has to be a reaching out to others—and to God—if true companionship is to flourish. The director knows that from God's point of view there is very little difference between him and his friend. He, for the time being, and only for the time being, has a word, a healing word. He knows that all the time he must be listening for the healing word from those who come to him for guidance.

One way of speaking about the difference between psychotherapy and spiritual direction is to say that spiritual direction is explicitly concerned with mutuality, grace, and worship.

First, the relationship between director and directed is one of essential equality and mutuality before God. As we have already seen, the person seeking direction must be able to relate to others, must be able to reach out, however fumblingly, to his brothers and sisters. Unless there is the openness (however small), a spiritual director is of little use. A closed-in person needs a different kind of expertise; that of the skilled therapist. There are, however, countless persons who hang together reasonably well, who want to pray more, love more, and *be* more. They turn to the Church—and often find no help.

This does not mean that God is not at work in us when we have no friends around to help us. It is a popular mistake to imagine that God somehow needs us. The wonderful thing is that, while he has no need of us, he still invites us to be co-workers with him. This I find comforting if a little unnerving because I want to be needed. This brings me to the second concern of spiritual direction: It explicitly places us in the order of grace. I am grateful that God is at work whether I am cooperative or not. Sometimes I feel so alienated from others and from the world that my only companion is God, and even that companionship seems stale and dry. Sometimes, when no ones seems to be of help in our spiritual pilgrimage, God is at work in our lonely depths pulling us through and preparing us for deeper relationships with others. I find that I am dealing with an alternating reality. There are times when the vertical relationship to God, experienced as sheer grace, has to be given priority over the horizontal relationship I have with others. Then the pendulum swings the other way.

Third, the context of spiritual direction must be one of adoration, expectancy, and commitment. Presumably, the last two are required in the therapeutic context as well, but adoration is peculiar to spiritual direction. For spiritual direction, at its heart, is liturgical. It is worship. It is adoration. It is waiting on God. This difference is crucial, for it places director and directed firmly within the realm of grace.

The therapist, the counselor, the psychiatrist can help us on our way. They can rescue us from particular blocks, get us back on our feet, can teach us to accept ourselves so that we can be on the move. But they cannot answer for us (nor would the best of them want to) those burning questions concerning the purpose and meaning for which we long. The spiritual guide cannot answer them either, but there is within the world of spiritual direction a conscious commitment to faith in God. The director and directed share in a community of faith with a common memory, a common hope, and a common longing.

The spiritual director's main concern is with our response to this longing and with our continual surrender to it. The director needs, therefore, above all, to be a person who prays, a person who knows the tradition (that which bears life), a person who is constantly open to his or her longings.

The director has been called "the disciplined wild man."[5] We should note that he is disciplined, not tamed. He is a pilgrim himself, a wounded healer (how that phrase keeps coming back). He does not set himself up as an expert. He sees himself as a companion to others, subject to the same hurts and temptations: Loneliness, self-contempt, moral ambiguity attack him as much as anyone else. Most of us have to live, from time to time, with that triple agony, an agony known by all who give spiritual direction.

Another way of understanding the difference between therapy and spiritual direction is to look at the Jesuit tradition. There has been an encouraging revival of Ignatian Studies, particularly as they effect spiritual direction in the Roman Catholic Church. St. Ignatius Loyola has much to teach us and his Exercises offer us first lessons for companions who wish to grow in the Spirit. Ignatius asks four fundamental questions about human existence. These questions help me understand the area and scope of spiritual direction as a response to my longing for God.

1. What is the focus of human existence? God! That is to say that

a human being's fundamental focus has, by definition, to be a religious one. Life is a matter of faith.

2. What is our purpose? To praise, to reverence, and to serve God. A human being is designed for worship and glory. A human being who does not worship is not yet human.

3. What is our destiny? Eternal life, faith in God, and an adoring intimacy with him are the means by which the Christian is given the power to overcome the tragedy of death.

4. How do we achieve eternal life? By playing the role God has given us. Direction is important for us in discerning our unique vocation and vocation as children of God. The good news of the gospel is proclaimed in spiritual direction: God made us and loves us to such a fantastic extent that he identifies utterly with our condition. Essentially, the director is a bearer of good news. It is the affirmation of that same faith of Julian of Norwich as she saw the world in the hands of God: "God made it, God loves it, God keeps it."

I wrote earlier that our longing for God is a longing for the real. It is a longing to Be with capital *B*. I think that is what Ignatius wanted. In fact, he wanted it so much that he sent his followers out to set the world aflame. He wanted all of us to be on fire with the glory of God. Ignatius and those like him confront me with my own questions: Am I sincere in wanting to respond to my longing for God, especially when I know and fear the revolutionary changes which may be involved?

My sincerity is often shaky, and I need you to reach out and help me break out of my imprisoning shell. Spiritual growth, which Louis Evely likens to that of lobsters, is exciting and painful. Lobsters grow too big for their shells and have to burst out of them and face the heat of the sun and the sting of the brine, exposing their tender flesh to the elements. We are meant for glory, which is being in all its fullness. It means really coming alive. Sometimes it is hard to bear. Like heat and light, it takes getting used to.

Both spiritual director and psychotherapist can prepare us for glory, and those of us who are neither therapists nor directors in any formal sense can help one another and guide one another as companions along the way. We can all learn what it means to bear one another's burdens. We can all share the mystery of being held together by another having faith in us. Christian companions not only believe in God, but also believe in one another. I need you to believe in me if I am to grow and live.

The so-called layperson (that is, the person who feels himself ignorant and incompetent: "I'm *only* a layman!") is often the one who can rescue the priest and the psychotherapist from their mind-spinning expertise. The layman may prevent the expert from falling into a state of megalomania at times—especially when the "expert" professes a subtle knowledge of humanity which is far beyond the poor layman's untrained sense, and believes it imperative that he or she preserve his or her secret knowledge from the uninitiated. Clergy, in general, are in the highly dangerous position of being, in the eyes of many, peddlers of dreams, traffickers in meaning. Indeed, that is part of their vocation. Spiritual guidance, however, is a vocation open to all, lay or ordained alike. The ministry of spiritual direction is not the special preserve of the clergy, and I suspect that there are countless lay people with frustrated vocations simply because of ignorance or lack of encouragement. There is a long tradition of holy men and women who have not been ordained, but who have served the Church as spiritual guides. Theirs is a tradition of quiet and unsung heroism. Now is the time to call out and recognize this neglected vocation. People who will respond to this call to companionship are sorely needed. Why? Because the Christian path is often painful. As Aeschylus reminded us: "Zeus has opened to mortal man a way of knowledge; he has ordained a sovereign decree—through suffering comes understanding." I would add that the God of Abraham, Isaac, and Jacob, the God of our Lord Jesus Christ, has opened to us a way of love; he has ordained a sovereign decree: die in response to our deepest longings, in which death is overcome and we begin to live in a liberating intimacy with God and with one another.

John V. Taylor ends his book *The Go-Between God*, with a wonderful example of the love of God coming to us in simple human contact when a person is willing to be with another in a moment of pain. Spiritual guidance is made of such moments. The story is common enough. Someone's husband is killed in a street accident. It happens all the time. The wife is stunned by the news; so much so that she sits transfixed on the sofa. She won't or can't move and soon her faraway lost look begins to embarrass and worry her family and the few friends who gather around to help. No one can reach her. Finally the teacher of one of the children drops by. She says nothing, but simply sits beside the stricken woman, puts her arm around her shoulders, and holds her close. Their cheeks meet and slowly the teacher, feeling the other's pain, begins to weep. The tears flow freely. After a while the wife begins to cry too and together they weep, the tears dropping onto their clasped hands.

John Taylor comments:

> That is the embrace of God, his kiss of life. That is the embrace of his mission, and of our intercession. And the Holy Spirit is the force in the straining muscles of an arm, the film of sweat between pressed cheeks, the mingled wetness on the backs of clasped hands. He is as close and as unobtrusive as that, and as irresistibly strong.[6]

This story struck chords in me because it is common. My own father dropped dead, suddenly and unexpectedly, on the street. He was fifty-one. For our family, too, the Holy Spirit came as the film of sweat between pressed cheeks. The art of arts is built upon such simplicity. Christian companionship consists in a simple response to such common events. I want you to be there for me and I want to be there for you.

4

Asking for Help
The Road to Freedom

*Am I, in the middle of my own struggles,
daring enough to ask for help, seek guidance,
cultivate friendships?*

This is a serious question in an age which highly values self-sufficiency. Shakespeare's Richard II in a poignant speech declares ironically that even he longs for friendship:

> Cover your heads and mock not flesh and blood
> With solemn reverence: throw away respect,
> Tradition, form and ceremonious duty,
> For you have but mistook me all this while:
> I live with bread like you, feel want,
> Taste grief, need friends.

Friendship is for men and women of flesh and blood who feel want and taste grief; the Christian belief is that God offers us his friendship and seeks ours.

The Christian believes that God is already at work in every human being—sometimes painfully, sometimes joyfully. God is always trying to reach us and bring us to himself. God does this primarily through his availability to us in Jesus Christ, who not only provides us with a pattern for living and growing, but is also our companion and savior. The question is how can I surrender myself to God in Christ and still be me? Indeed, this is the question I ask myself with regard to my closest friends. It is possible for me to love them and be loved by them in such a way that we are truly one and, at the same time, truly distinct and separate? How do I love others, love God without being swallowed up? My fear of being swallowed makes me hesitate to ask for help, seek guidance, cultivate friendships.

The more aware I become of my longing for God, the more I am fearful about being engulfed. Indeed, the more aware I am of the world about me, the less of a grip I seem to have on myself. That is why spiritual direction can be dangerous business. It is, in some sense, a placing of myself in the hands of an other. The possibility of exploitation, of psychological and spiritual tyrannies is obvious, but I tend to allow my fears of exploitation and tyranny get the better of me. The fear then becomes an excuse not to enter into a relationship at all. Furthermore, if I once place myself in the hands of an other, I will set in motion a course of events beyond my control. I will learn real things, become more aware of life's lights and shadows. This is, deep down, what I want, but there is something in me that continues to resist my deepest longings. Part of me wants to be left alone. Another part wants to be taken up and told exactly what to do. Between the me who wants to be self-sufficient and autonomous and the me who wants to be told all the answers, there is a me who wants to relate to others in a free and responsible way. There is within each one of us a double desire to tyrannize or to be tyrannized, which is directly linked to our desire for absolute knowledge, for the certainty that is beyond question. There are no lengths to which human beings will not go to be secure.

Security is often bought at the expense of growth and adventure. Which will it be? The security of a life where nothing changes, nothing grows, or the risk and adventure as part of what it means to be a pilgrim people? The spiritual life requires risk because the new is always breaking in. The old is always having to shift and accommodate to new insights, to new perspectives. The modern phrase for this is "consciousness-raising," and my daring to ask for spiritual guidance involves me in this willingness to have my view of reality expanded and, on occasions, exploded.

Heightened awareness sometimes threatens and always questions my sense of who I am. In extreme cases a person can be thoroughly disoriented by an experience of the new breaking into his life. When someone is struck by a thunderbolt of the Spirit, as Paul was on the Damascus road, his sense of who he is suffers enormously. He is, like Paul, blinded by the experience, and he needs a guide or a friend to take him by the hand. New insights, however small, new data, however trivial, have to be absorbed, integrated (or suppressed) by the person who is open to adventure. In classic adventure stories there are mountains to climb, jungles to struggle through, forces of evil to overcome. The overcoming of these obstacles does something that changes the participants. The adventurer undergoes a kind of rebirth in the passing through many dangers. The more cataclysmic the events, the more traumatic is the rebirth. New identities have to be forged and old habits, discarded. Heightened awareness, new vision, raised-consciousness frequently produce crisis. They invite change. They threaten the deepest and most insecure parts of ourselves. This is why spiritual growth is such a delicate matter and why spiritual direction requires deep sensitivity. But as I move forward in pilgrimage the question changes from, "Dare I ask for guidance?" to "Dare I *not* ask for it?"

But what will this guidance entail? Will it guarantee me some stability and security? I know that can't be so because I have no way of giving such a guarantee to others. One of the things we learn when we dare to ask for help, seek guidance, and cultivate friendships is that it is a two-way street. When I ask for help, there is an implicit understanding that, when the time comes, I will be asked for help in return. This understanding does not exist in the spirit of a kind of negotiated treaty between two persons. It is there because mutuality is implicit from the start. The relationship is, by its very nature, two-way.

Whether I am giving or receiving spiritual direction, I am faced with the question of how tough I want the encounter to be. If I am the director, the question is how far I should go in stretching and challenging the other person. If I'm on the receiving end, I ask how far I want or need to be pushed. How far, for example, should those who come for spiritual direction be encouraged to escape from their own darkness? If I come for direction I expect to be taken seriously. I know that I need to be challenged and pushed. Once I have dared to make the commitment to the direction relationship, I want something more than a pat on the head. I also want something considerably less than a bludgeoning! I find that a too easy acceptance of who I am can be little more than a shallow expression of concern on the part of a director. Yet a too rigorous approach can lead to despair. At some points, the director will be pushing me towards more awareness. At others, he or she will need to nurse my damaged and wounded sense of self. On occasions I need gentle handling. At other times, a serious confrontation is in order. A good director will know when to push and when to hold back.

Spiritual direction involves the transformation of our identity because "it does not yet appear what we shall be." Direction demands the surrender of the self to rediscover ourselves in Christ. This pattern of surrender is sometimes almost unbearable. New awareness of a particularly explosive nature can cause deep disturbances where the connections between the person, the world, and others seem, for a time, completely severed. It is at such moments that the nurturing environment provided by the Christian community plays a vital part in a person's spiritual growth. My experience at seminary in England comes to mind when the Christian community carried me through such a period of deep inner disturbance.

Nowadays people are peculiarly vulnerable to spiritual upheavals. Many problems and ailments in spiritual direction spring from a raised-consciousness with its corresponding threat to a settled sense of identity, purpose, and destiny. Many people have gone through a process of heightened awareness and the necessary stress which it entails, but have not yet moved forward into a process of reintegration, the reforging of a new identity. Often technicians of the psyche offer experiences that genuinely deepen a person's awareness of themselves and their world. What they do not provide (at least, as a rule) is an ongoing community to sustain the person through a period of upheaval. This state of affairs should not, however, be seen merely as a problem, still less a tragedy. It is also an opportunity for spiritual growth.

An experience of heightened awareness can be a sort of breakthrough in the soul, not unlike speaking in tongues. It doesn't make much sense unless there is an interpreter or companion and unless it happens within the broadening context of a worshiping community. Here is another problem-opportunity. Heightened awareness not only threatens our present understanding of who we are, it can also weaken our sense of belonging. Most people, in one way or another, discover their identity by belonging to a group or to a community. In fact, many are so desperate that they will surrender themselves to a group, a party, or a church simply in order to have that sense of being somebody that belonging brings.

Heightened awareness (as both problem and opportunity) often brings in its wake disturbing things that need to be dealt with in spiritual direction. If they are not faced honestly they can cause deep spiritual harm. For example, I am sometimes overcome by a sense of isolation and loneliness which can often be mistaken for individuality. I have often been tempted to say such things as: "There is no one quite like me, no one really understands!" Or "With my insights I am not subject to the conventions, laws, and customs of other people." Or "No one is wise or holy enough to understand my peculiar problems." This attitude, of course, only serves to increase my sense of isolation. I begin to enter a lonely and unreal world. I treat my friends abominably.

The pendulum often swings from spiritual arrogance to an unrealistic conviction of my own worthlessness and inadequacy. Heightened awareness, after all, invites me to see everything, warts and all. I might be able to get away with regarding sin as an illusion, but self-hate, and the overwhelming sense of mortality, are real enough. This swing of the pendulum between arrogance and self-contempt is a pattern that can often be discerned in the apparently intelligent and self-assured.

Self-knowledge, then, always brings with it a certain amount of insecurity. For one thing, it will not allow me to project my sense of evil onto others. As I get to know myself, I become increasingly and uncomfortably aware that all hatred is self-hatred. At the same time, I have to acknowledge the good impulses. But which am I really: good or evil? These conflicting forces coexist within me. Who am I really? Which is the real me? What is the focus of, the clue to, my real identity? The self soon becomes a battlefield between good and bad impulses, as St. Paul was brilliantly aware: "For I do not do the good I want, but the evil I do not want is what I do" (Rom. 7:19).

Spiritual direction is often hard for imaginative and clever people to receive because their minds are easily tempted by new ideas and images and they can be mesmerized by too much information, too much data. They are overloaded with images and ideas and these undermine their sense of identity. The sources which used to nourish their sense of identity seem to have dried up.

Heightened awareness of the gospel does two things: it exalts and it humbles at the same time. It is the double pattern of the saints and mystics: joy and sorrow, glory and suffering, resurrection and death. Heightened awareness of the gospel raises the problem and opportunity of obedience to Christ and this obedience to him increasingly becomes a terrible threat: We are invited to be a disciple of Jesus, and look what happened to him! This is the difference between spiritual direction and secular therapy, this explicit commitment to Jesus. It is in him that we find out who we really are. Identity is always revealed and given in relationship, and true relationships always make us more aware and evoke in us loving iconoclasm with regard to the way we see ourselves. Our self-image is often shattered by the loving demands of our relationships.

The spiritual director needs to bear witness to the fact that no one else but Christ can tell us who we are. No one! Yet there are plenty of people who would like to tell us who we are and what to do. It is precisely in moments of crisis that we are the most susceptible to blind obedience to authority. In situations of conflict or crisis our awareness of ourselves and others is diminished considerably. When we are threatened, however mildly, there is a tendency to caricature our enemies and ourselves. A new sense of self emerges from the fantasy world within us, and for a while we feel comfortable and safe because we have identified our enemy and are at home with our own kind.

Adam Curle, in his book *Mystics and Militants*, suggests that there are two ways in which we come to a sense of ourselves. The first is by a commitment to a way of life which continually stretches us, makes us more aware; the second is easier and involves our finding a group to which we can belong. Most people choose the easier route because a strong sense of identity through belonging to a particular group saves one of the expensive process of growing more and more aware of oneself and one's surroundings. A mystic or militant is one who is committed to the harder way and who resists self-definition in terms of a group. He or she is, therefore, less tied to the status quo than the person who derives his or her sense of identity from belonging, for example, to a sect or a political party. The mystic and the militant exercise a powerful influence on others and it is often those who need the easier route who surrender their identity to charismatic leaders of either the mystical or revolutionary type. But don't we all need to feel that we belong? Surely not all belonging is bad. Curle is not denying the kind of belonging that is based on love, but rather the kind of belonging that is based on group cohesiveness. There is a world of difference between someone belonging to the Nazi party and someone belonging to the Christian community.

The Christian, as he or she grows in the Spirit, cannot and must not avoid new insights. To be unaware is to deny our very being, to repress who we really are. When we do that things go bad, life turns sour. In the end, to be unaware is to be enslaved by a false sense of self.

Spiritual direction takes place within the supportive context of a believing community, which, in turn, understands itself as the guardian of a life-bearing tradition. Within such an environment I can dare to look at new things even if I am sometimes disturbed by what I see. It is at such moments, when the new is emerging in my life, that I wonder what will become of me.

This is the point at which I need the support that spiritual direction at its best provides. In the Eastern tradition this state of disturbance which the new occasions is called "between dreams" and is an opportunity for spiritual growth. The idea is this: Life is a very important dream made up of images which structure reality for us. From time to time we wake up and, much to our horror, we open our eyes and find darkness. There is nothing that seems to hold life together. There are no longer any images and structures to help us make sense of things. We panic and try to get back to sleep as soon as possible and recover the old dream. If we are willing to wait in the darkness "between dreams" a larger and wider reality appears and life's dream takes on richer images and more liberating structures. It's often at a place such as "between dreams" that a guide, a friend, or spiritual director can wait with us in the dark place until a new way of looking at things emerges for us. Many a marriage, for example, turns sour and dies precisely at the point of its greatest possible growth, when old images and structures have to be discarded and the new have yet to emerge.

It takes considerable courage to wait in the dark between dreams and I don't know how it can be done without the grace of God and a struggling determination to trust him in the darkness. Nor can I envisage being able to wait for the coming of light without the supportive framework of friendship and community. The Christian "heightened awareness" is made possible by the presence of a fellowship of fellow pilgrims.

The Christian heightens his or her awareness by sharing in what Paul calls "the mind of Christ." Prayer is an adventurous descent into that mind where, by the power of the Holy Spirit, our self-consciousness is transfigured into Christ-consciousness. It is inevitably a way of sacrifice and self-surrender, a way not unlike the traditional call to monasticism. It is a creative way of poverty, chastity, and obedience—poverty, because it means being truly poor before God; chastity, because it involves a single-minded devotion to him; obedience, because our single-minded attention will be manifested in specific acts of love. This threefold way is one of submission, of sacrifice and surrender for the sake of the more abundant life. The three traditional monastic vows provide us with some clues about the way in which all Christians are called to respond to the freedom offered them in Christ. They are the marks of Christ himself and subsequently the marks of those who follow him. Poverty, chastity, and obedience are also the marks of a good spiritual guide and friend of the soul.

What could these virtues mean to us—men and women, unmarried and married? Poverty, which is not to be confused with penury (grinding poverty), is a virtue and "means the recognition that in the most real sense the world is mine, whoever owns it in the narrow technical sense. Poverty is thus the ability to enjoy the world to the full because I am not anxious about losing a bit of it or acquiring a bit of it. Poverty takes pleasure in a thing because it is, and not because it can be possessed."[1] Poverty as a virtue, then, involves a contemplative stance before the world. We look. We give things our close attention. It is then that we can enjoy them unambiguously. Such enjoyment involves an essentially meditative attitude, and meditation is the art of letting go and becoming unpossessive about people and things. Poverty, in this sense, provides the context in which I can dare to ask for guidance when I need it.

Poverty is also a latent inner resource which knows that both success and failure, as the world understands them, have nothing to do with personal worth. As Harry Williams writes, "Poverty understands that I am not my success and that I am not my failure but that both are no more than food which can nourish what I really am—a being who has nothing and yet possesses all things."[2] So, poverty is a prerequisite for the kind of loving which is neither possessive nor cannibalistic. Poverty will not allow me to project all my needs and fantasies onto another. I have to learn to receive, to accept the other person for whom he or she really is. Finally, our poverty is to be seen in the light of the poverty of God—the self-emptying One—and in our self-surrender, we discover that "man is never a mere cul-de-sac. He is a road to what is infinitely greater than himself."[3] When someone is poor in this sense of the word, I can dare approach him and ask for help because this kind of poverty of spirit creates around itself an open and free space.

Chastity, like poverty, is basically a positive virtue and is the mark of a free man or woman in Christ. First, there is intellectual chastity, which is the expression of that "inner necessity to separate what is of value from what is worthless."[4] This kind of chastity enables us to enjoy the world more because it brings with it an inner power of discernment. To enjoy the world fully we need to be able to tell the authentic from the false. Jargon is a sin against intellectual chastity. Why? Because "it is an attempt to sound clever when you have nothing to say."[5]

On the emotional level, chastity is seen as the attempt to be loyal to the deepest and the best that is in us, while more superficial feelings crash around inside. Emotional chastity prevents us from being sloppy and sentimental for the sake of feeling good for a brief time. Harry Williams refers to George MacDonald's two silly young people: "They had a feeling, or a feeling had them, till another feeling came and took its place. When a feeling was there, they felt it would never go; when it was gone, they felt as if it had never been; when it returned, they felt as if it had never gone."[6] A good spiritual director has that reassuring stability that is the result of emotional chastity. It is a single-mindedness which, like poverty, creates the space where growth can happen.

Sins against chastity are sins because they involve the abdication of personal identity. I give up being responsible for who I am when I surrender to the emotions of the moment. Surrender to a temporary emotion, or even a constant one, involves an impoverishment of what it is to be human. I *become* my passion for power, for him, or for her. When I do that I am lost.

So chastity is a matter of faith, a matter of discovering—often painfully—what my basic commitments really are and being true to them. Emotional chastity is the pursuit of wholeness. Intellectual chastity is the shifting of experience "so that we can be enriched by it instead of being diminished or destroyed."[7]

Harry Williams ends a sermon on chastity with these words: "The flesh can never be made Word, but the Word is forever being made flesh and to know that is to find your true self. It is to be chaste."[8] And who is the Word? The Word to us about ourselves is Jesus Christ. To be chaste in the sense I have been using the word (which is not to deny its conventional meaning) is to be utterly attentive to him as the focus and source of our identity. To grow in him is to grow up to be ourselves.

Obedience, like chastity, is a matter of loyalty to the deepest stirrings within us. It is not a matter of following a route of safety. Williams quotes the famous obituary of a member of the Washington establishment in the thirties: "He had no ideas. He wasn't a nuisance."[9] Is that going to be my epitaph?

The best model I know in the contemporary world for obedience is that of the creative artist. The artist, to be true to himself, has to be obedient to the vision he has been given. Obedience is the key to the Christian understanding of what a human being is. To be human is to respond to God in Christ—to say Yes! Obedience has, of course, a social and religious aspect. The former is the response in love to the needs and concerns of others. Social obedience, however, is "not simply or chiefly submission to external authority; it is a way of being loyal to yourself and of enabling others to do the same."[10] The religious aspect of obedience has to do with the deeper self, with the need of the self to transcend itself. It is the Yes! to that within me which is more me than myself. To be fully human, we have to acknowledge the mystery within ourselves. St. Catherine of Genoa said: "My me is God, nor do I know my selfhood save in him." There, in a nutshell, is what a spiritual guide can show me.

He or she places my sometimes wild thrashing about looking for myself in the ever-widening context of God's love. This love has specific shape and content in Jesus Christ. I discover that I become more me when my life is shaped and formed by him. Only by being obedient to God and to nothing and no one less, can I be liberated from lesser obediences: the slavery of moods, emotions, and preferences.

The way of poverty, wherein we own all things; the way of chastity, wherein we love all things; the way of obedience, wherein we reign with Christ, is the charter of human liberation. We, therefore, have nothing to fear from the heightening of awareness, or the raising of consciousness. I need not be hesitant about asking for help, seeking guidance, cultivating friendship in a focused and intentional way. It is, after all, the way God made me. He created me for relationship. He made me in such a way that reaching out to others is a genuine expression of who I am. My identity is secure, "it is hidden with Christ in God," it is known by the One who made me and who loves me. A spiritual director is one who is willing to be my companion (one who shares the same bread) in my battle to surrender to the One who knows who I really am and who loves me all the way through.

Charles Williams brilliantly describes the painful battle for possession of the human heart. Sybil, in *The Greater Trumps,* had done battle with "principalities and powers," so that the inner strength and peace which was now hers "had not been easily reached."

> That sovereign state, the inalienable heritage of man, had been in her, as in all, falsely mortgaged to the intruding control of her own greedy desires. Even when the true law had been discovered, when she knew that she had the right and the power to possess all things, on the one condition that she herself was possessed, even then her freedom to yield herself had been won by many conflicts.[11]

Our freedom comes in the yielding to God and finding that the miracle happens: perfect unity with perfect identity. This is another way of saying, "My me is God, nor do I know my selfhood save in him." My fear of loss is swallowed up in the promise and anticipation of a new and fuller life. My deepest questions are answered by the love of God. I need not fear being engulfed or swallowed up. My friends over and over again are the gracious emissaries of a loving God when they reach out to me without greediness or possessiveness, when like God and godlike they set me free to be myself.

5

All Daring Confidence in God
Using God's Gifts

*Do I really believe that my life comes to me as
a gift and that there is in me a terrific thing?*

The work of spiritual direction rests on a mighty act of faith. It places everything we are in the context of the love of God. This is where we begin and end. This may sound obvious and even simpleminded, but it needs to be said because even the most committed believer sometimes forgets. The terrific thing, which we identify with the Holy Spirit, gets lost, or so covered over with grime and soot as to be almost unrecognizable.

Spiritual direction is God's work. This cannot be overemphasized. When as a director I forget the sovereignty of God, I easily fall into the trap of believing that I am indispensable. I am often confused about what part I am supposed to play in the mystery of another person's spiritual formation. I am faced with a dilemma. On the one hand, I believe that the work of spiritual direction is all God's work; on the other, I believe that he chooses to work through frail human instruments. I ask myself what gifts are needed for this art of arts? If spiritual direction is all God's work, then what are the gifts or qualities required in a spiritual director?

On one level, we have no gifts at all, at least none that we possess as a right. We are nothing of ourselves, and we have nothing with which to negotiate with God. Yet, as we have seen, the art of spiritual direction presupposes God's free use of fragile human beings to accomplish his purpose. There is no way we can straitjacket the Holy Spirit no matter how much we would sometimes like to. The Holy Spirit is the bearer of gifts and these gifts are sometimes lavished in peculiar places. Nevertheless, gifts which are believed to have come from the Holy Spirit have to be tested. It is of little use, and sometimes even dangerous, to claim that one is gifted in a certain way unless that gift is recognized by a group of others who create space so that one can exercise it. There is nothing sadder than a person who imagines that he or she has a gift but is suffering from a delusion. Florence Foster Jenkins, many years ago, gave public concerts because she thought she had a beautiful voice. She was rich enough to stage these events and her rendition of the Queen of the Night opening aria from Mozart's *Magic Flute* left her audience aching with laughter. It is a funny and a sad story of a person whose fantasy about her gifts severed any connection with the real state of affairs.

In a less spectacular way than the case of Florence Foster Jenkins, there are those who fancy themselves as gifted in matters of the spiritual life and who offer their services to the world. This can take a sinister turn if people are duped by a self-appointed guru's own estimation of himself.

When it comes to the issue of spiritual direction we are not left without criteria by which to judge a person's giftedness. We stand in a long tradition and there are distinguishing marks of a Christian spiritual director.

A spiritual director makes no claims at all. The gift is recognized through the slow process of persons seeking him or her out of counsel or advice. Often the person they sought is puzzled. "Why are these people coming to me? I have no special qualifications." It is at that point that such a person can be put in touch with a long and honorable tradition and begin to learn about those who have preceded him or her. Being in touch with this tradition is a great comfort and safeguard to the spiritual director. It helps to resolve the dilemma which was mentioned earlier. It is all God's work, and such gifts that we have been given are for that work and that alone.

In any discussion of gifts we must begin with the affirmation that God's first gift to us is our unique and irreplaceable self, and it is that self which God chooses to use in spiritual guidance. It is the "terrific thing," my deepest self, enlivened by the Holy Spirit. It is a miracle of grace that all that we are (warts and all) is capable of being transformed into gift. With the sense of our giftedness comes also the sense of our limitations. A few years ago I spent thirty-one days in solitude. That experience taught me that acceptance of limitation and weakness goes along with the affirmation of giftedness. The solitude showed me my weaknesses. Worst of all, I came to feel utterly useless; but it was only when I came face to face with my own uselessness that God began to use me.

There is, then, no way we can take a list of gifts and go down it and check off the ones we think we have *unless* we are clear about the greatest gift of all, which is God's gift of himself to us in Jesus Christ. He is the One who enables each of us to be and become who we are. God can and does use to his glory the apparently ungifted. And this is very important for us to grasp in an age of "experts" who have all the "qualifications." In this particular art the instrument that is used is not a set of skills or techniques, but, rather, our own fragile selves.

As a Christian, I understand that God's first gift to me is myself. God enables me to say, "I am." That might seem very commonplace, but the verb *to be* is not as easily understood as we might suppose at first. To say I AM is to claim something godlike about oneself. "God said to Moses, 'I AM WHO I AM.' and he said, 'Say this to the people of Israel, "I AM has sent me to you"' " (Ex. 3:14). God invites me to say, "I am." This is his great gift to me. This giftedness in the Spirit has a double aspect. God, in giving himself to me, gives me back to myself. Dante describes the souls in heaven shining back to God with the divine splendor and saying "I am!" And Gregory of Nyssa (c. 330–c. 395) understood beautifully the way in which God invites us to be co-creators of ourselves with him when he said: "We are indeed in a sense our own fathers when through freely accepted discipline we give birth to ourselves." In my relationship to God (focused and centered in prayer) I experience the mystery of God continually giving me back to myself. This is the way I am formed, and the experience is not always pleasant because, in order for me to be me, I have to be committed to the free development of other persons. In order for me to be me, you have to be you. Even my own power to respond to God is a gift because I have no existence through my own agency. Only God exists from himself (*a se*). Thomas Merton became very excited when he discovered this basic Christian doctrine (the Aseity of God). God and only God exists through his own agency. As far as I am concerned everything is gift, and the first gift I receive is myself. "His gifts are good," writes St. Augustine, "and the sum of them is my own self."[1] But I cannot be me without you and you cannot be you without me. This means that our gifts are given us within and for the benefit of others. In other words, our gifts can only be understood within the fellowship of a human community. As "members one of another" a double responsibility is laid upon us. The first is to nurture and use our gifts without pride or self-consciousness. The second is to encourage others to use theirs.

There is nothing that preceded God's gift. To grasp that (or, at least, to catch a glimpse of it) is to have entered the mystery of life in God in the face of which prayer and spiritual companionship need neither justification nor explanation. It is to see that our formation as human beings is a matter of vocation and grace and not of essence or of right.

In our movement into the mystery of God everything that has happened to us is potential gift: our wounds, our disappointments, our idiosyncrasies, and our failures. This is not to glorify pain and sorrow, but to affirm that such things can be transformed into gift. The recovered alcoholic has the gift of speaking to other alcoholics in a way which a nonalcoholic cannot. The woman who has suffered a nervous breakdown has the terrible gift of knowing what total mental collapse is like and can listen sympathetically to others under stress. The man for whom sexuality is a persistent and unresolved problem can minister to others in a way in which a person who has "no problems" cannot. All these people have peculiar gifts which those who have been neither tested nor stretched do not have.

The Christian assumes that everything that we are and that has happened to us is capable of being transfigured into gift. The danger in a somewhat cynical age is that all these potential gifts can easily be dismissed as neuroses. This dismissal is insidious because it helps to keep us trapped inside ourselves. It is hard for us to see that our hurts and wounds are, potentially at least, gifts. It is not difficult to understand why some people fall into despair when their hurt has no outlet through which it might be transformed into gift.

The consequence of the Fall is self-contemplation. We are "curved in on ourselves" in a terrible kind of inwardness which blinds us both to our own gifts and to the gifts of others.

The Christian friend of the soul understands that self-emptying is required for the manifestation of gifts and that the proper use of our talents is to be patterned after the way in which the Holy Spirit works. The Spirit is reticent, deferential, and anonymous in that he is always pointing to, bearing witness to the Son. The use of our gifts requires reverence for others, part of which involves joy in hearing and telling the good of others.

About giftedness, Meister Eckhart (c. 1260–1327) wrote,

> God gives no gift, God never has given any gift, in order that anyone would have the gift and rest content with it. Rather, all the gifts that he has ever given, in heaven and on earth, were given in view of his single purpose, to give *one* gift, which is himself. With all these other gifts he wants to prepare us now for the gift which is himself; and all the works he has brought about in heaven and on earth were done simply to enable him to perform one work, namely to make himself blessed in making us blessed. This is why I say, in all gifts and works we must learn to see God, not let ourselves be content with anything, not allow ourselves to settle down with anything. In this life there is no settling down for us in any way, and there never was for any man, however far he may have progressed.[2]

Having emphasized that all is potential gift, including failures, it nevertheless remains that the tradition of this art of arts presupposes that spiritual direction is a peculiar and distinct vocation. Furthermore, it points to certain qualities desirable in a spiritual director. What are these qualities? A look at the tradition can help us.

One of the places where the tradition of spiritual direction is most honored and preserved is in Eastern Orthodoxy. There are, in the Eastern Church, four simple requirements for a spiritual guide. The first is love: not any kind of love, but an openness and readiness to accept another into one's heart. It is a love that takes time and is open to the possible anguish involved. Christianity has often been called the school of love and the spiritual director understands himself or herself as committed to a long apprenticeship which

involves both an intellectual as well as an emotional involvement
in the art of loving. Hence the spiritual director is by definition a
lover who holds his or her friends in the love of God in constant
intercession. To say that the first requirement is love is saying a
great deal more than our adopting a sentimental attitude. When the
Christian loves, he or she is sharing in a divine activity, for love is
the work of the Holy Spirit.

The second requirement is discernment. This requirement is the
heart of spiritual direction. Suffice it to say here that discernment
is a charism (a gift) of the Spirit. John Climacus in the sixth century
wrote his *Ladder of Divine Ascent*. There are thirty steps in all and
the twenty-sixth is discernment. The first requirement in discernment is to thoroughly know oneself. If I am to be truly discerning
I have to be aware of my own sinfulness and silliness and, at the
same time, through what the Eastern tradition beautifully calls "the
gift of tears," be aware of the amazing and forgiving love of God
available to me at all times. To discern is to be both penitential and
joyful at the same time: penitential because we discern how far we
have all fallen short of the glory of God; joyful because the glory
still outshines our failure to honor it. Discernment is the gift of
reading hearts. The great example in scripture is described in Jesus's encounter with the woman at the well in St. John's Gospel:

> Jesus said to her, "Go, call your husband, and come here." The
> woman answered him, "I have no husband." Jesus said to her,
> "You are right in saying, 'I have no husband'; for you have had
> five husbands, and he whom you now have is not your husband;
> this you said truly." The woman said to him, "Sir, I perceive that
> you are a prophet."
>
> John 4: 16–20

There are warnings that the gift of discernment must always be
exercised within the context of love. Without love, discernment can
be destructive.

The third requirement is patience. This may seem obvious, but
it is no easy thing to sit still and wait. We are tempted to make quick
judgments and are either too relaxed or too harsh in our dealings
with others. John Cassian (c. 360–435) said wisely, "Severity and
harshness never change anyone." It was an impatient and unsym-

pathetic confessor who told Thomas Merton that he certainly had no vocation to either the priesthood or the religious life! Patience is the courage to be still and wait.

The fourth requirement is utter frankness and honesty on both sides of the relationship. It requires a naked trust which will set the tone of a relationship and will enable both to go very deep, beyond mere reaction to the impulses, drives, and energies that stir us up.

Finally, the Eastern tradition demands that the spiritual director be willing to embrace solitude and cultivate detachment so that he or she may be more available to what God, the Holy Spirit, is doing in the individual human heart.

In the Western tradition, St. John of the Cross (1542–1591) was one of the greatest spiritual directors. He was utterly convinced of the necessity of spiritual direction. Indeed he went so far as to write: "God is desirous that the government and direction of every man should be undertaken by another man." This may seem strange and even harsh but he is insisting that we need one another and that God has so ordained things that we grow in the Spirit only through the frail instrumentality of one another. He writes: "A soul which remains alone without a master is like a burning coal which is alone. It will grow colder rather than hotter."

A spiritual director, then, is first and foremost someone who is burning with love, like a red-hot coal. He also knows instinctively the source and origin of this fire. In his *Living Flame*, St. John beautifully expresses the fundamental truth of spiritual direction:

> The Holy Spirit is the principal agent and mover of souls and never loses care for them; and the directors themselves are not agents but only instruments to lead souls . . . in the rule of faith and in the law of God according to the spirituality that God is giving to each one. Let them not, therefore, merely aim at guiding a soul according to their own way and the manner suited to themselves, but let them see if they know the way by which God is leading the soul. And if they know it not, let them leave the soul in peace and not disturb it.[3]

Spiritual direction, therefore, requires a great deal of sensitivity to others. It is a work of collaboration between us and God in whom we are both free and freeing instruments. Self-knowledge is very important. We need to know our capacities, limitations, and competencies.

Spiritual direction is a work of fearsome responsibility. St. John has some harsh words for incompetent directors: "It is a thing of no small weight, and no light crime, to cause the soul to lose inestimable blessings by counseling it to go out of its way. . . . And thus one who rashly errs, being under an obligation to give reliable advice . . . shall not go unpunished, by reason of the harm he has done. For the business of God has to be undertaken with great circumspection, and with eyes wide open."[4]

St. John's list of requirements are very similar to those found in the Eastern tradition. The first is love, to which he adds courtesy. This sounds, alas, strangely old-fashioned, but it implies a tender respect for the person in one's care. It involves a quiet and confident acceptance of the other. "The holier the confessor, the gentler they are and the less easily scandalized." From this holiness of life comes the director's authority which is accepted without hesitation because all affectation is absent. Detachment is also very important. In modern psychological terms St. John was well aware of problems of transference and projection. He knew how easy it is to be captivated or infatuated by another. When that happens both freedom and authority are lost.

Finally, St. John of the Cross insisted on theological competence, since this was the area where he was most open to criticism. He was always careful to point out that his mystical experiences were undergirded by sound teaching. Concerning incompetent clergy he wrote, "Such persons have no knowledge of what is meant by spirituality. They offer a great insult—great irreverence to God, by laying their coarse hands where God is working."

Spiritual direction, for St. John, was a means by which the Church would be reformed. He understood our yearning for holiness and was impatient with half measures and with mediocrity. The formation and transformation of persons in the power of the Spirit was the fundamental vocation of the Church. It was part of his missionary identity and apostolic activity. The spiritual director is an apostle helping to form other apostles.

Another in the Western tradition was St. Francis de Sales (1567–1622). He adds his voice to the witness of St. John of the Cross. In his *Introduction to the Devout Life,* he emphasizes that a spiritual director should be both loving and learned. Love is not enough. It must be an informed love. St. Francis was well aware that because the relationship is personal it cannot be reduced to rules. We may be loving, learned, and wise, but these are no guarantees of success. The relationship between the director and the directed is a supernatural one. God is at work in it and St. Francis states: "There are fewer than can be imagined who are capable of this office." This is not very encouraging and would be depressing but for the fact that the Spirit is already at work in our hearts which need to sit still and be quiet, waiting for the Spirit's leading. In fact, according to St. Francis, the director rarely takes initiative. He follows and listens: "I leave in God's hands the primary work that cuts back useless shoots."[5]

The director, then, should occasionally explain and give counsel, sometimes restrain or encourage, and console often. St. Francis also gives sound advise to the directed. Be open. Give a sincere account of yourself, both good and bad without pretense, so that the good in you will be fortified and the bad remedied.

Perhaps the most important of all spiritual directors of the seventeenth century is Dom Augustine Baker (1575–1644). He had a wonderful gift of silent attractiveness in a noisy and turbulent age. Once Father Baker (a Roman Catholic Benedictine monk) was staying at the house of his Catholic friend Mr. Philip Fursdon. The whole household was Catholic except for Fursdon's mother-in-law, who was a devout Protestant. She was continually pestered and badgered by her Catholic relations and visiting clergy. Father Baker was gentle and never questioned her about her religion. His reticence puzzled her.

> Discoursing with Father Baker after dinner about ordinary matters . . . she asked him why he . . . should treat with her after a fashion wholly different from all his brothers; for they almost deafened her with their continual clamorous disputes, but he never made the least attempt to persuade her to agree in belief with him. She told him . . . the devout life he led and his edifying carriage sufficiently witnessed that this behavior of his to her proceeded from some other principle, which she desired to know.[6]

Father Baker's first principle was that the Holy Spirit is the only sure guide and master. This is based on the conviction that in every human being there is a "certain propension to seek God . . . which is a kind of natural devotion. . . . Now when divine grace adjoins itself to such good propensions it promotes and increases them, rectifying what is amiss in them . . . but it doth not alter the complexion itself, but conducts souls in spiritual ways suitable to their several dispositions by an almost infinite variety of patterns and fashions, yet all tending to the same general ends, which is the union of our spirits with God by perfect love."[7] Two qualities required in a spiritual director are the ability to reverence the infinite variety of human beings and the proper humility and understanding of the difficulty of the task.

> The instructor, therefore, is to behave himself towards them all according to the quality and needs of each spirit, always remembering that his office is not to teach his own way, nor indeed any determinate way of prayer but to instruct his disciples how they may themselves find out the way proper for them, by observing themselves what doth good and what causeth harm to their spirits; in a word, that he is only God's usher, and must lead souls in God's way and not his own.[8]

In describing the spiritual director as "God's usher," Father Baker strikes the right note for our understanding and our use of God's gifts to aid us as we struggle and learn together in this school of love. This Benedictine monk stands in the long tradition of spiritual guides whose strength is derived from the sure faith that life comes to them as sheer gift. They are able to discern in another person the terrific thing and to worship God in another human person without confusing the creature with the Creator.

6

Spiritual Direction as a Work of the Imagination

One of the most wonderful gifts we receive from a spiritual director or a friend of the soul is that of a new perspective. He or she is able to stir up our imagination so that we not only view the past differently, but also allow the future to be pregnant with new and exciting possibilities. Sometimes all it takes to bring about the miracle of new hope is a tiny shift of perspective, like a painter seeing a whole new landscape merely by changing the position of his easel. A spiritual friend can do that for us. A word from a friend, in causing a small shift in perspective, can sometimes get us off the treadmill of fatalism and despair where nothing new ever happens. But it must be said that the reverse is also true. Words are like barbs and can wound if aimed directly at a tender spot. An unkind word can stir up in us a host of negative images. A slight shift in perspective can also set us *on* a treadmill. There is, therefore, a struggle for true perspective in each one of us: a battle of images. What kind of images want to take possession of my imagination? They might be images of hopelessness, nastiness, and despair. How are they to be resisted? Indeed, can they be resisted? The most intense part of spiritual combat, for me, is with the many images that struggle to possess me.

I am, for example, often dissatisfied with the kind of person I am. I have a low self-image. The dissatisfaction comes when I see the gap between what I believe about the world and the sort of person I really am. Too often my behavior flatly denies my beliefs. When I am unloving, consumed with dark thoughts, angry and resentful with friends and family, I am falling short of the image of myself which my beliefs demand of me. There is then a struggle between two images: between the person I am meant to be and the person I am. It is often an act of simple and unaffected friendship which rescues me from myself. I tend to get lost in my imagination.

What exactly is imagination anyway? Shouldn't I try to repress it? Won't an active imagination encourage me to live completely in a fantasy world of my own making? Didn't the early Desert Fathers give repeated warnings about the unreliability of the imagination (phantasia)? My imagination, however, won't be repressed, no matter how hard I try. My only way through is to find ways in which it can be channeled to good purpose. David Baily Harned gives a helpful definition of what is meant by imagination when it is thus channeled. It is

> the sum of all the resources within us that we employ to form accurate images of the self and its world. The imagination is concerned with the discovery of potentiality and new possibilities, with what is not yet, but only because it is oriented first of all toward actuality.[1]

Imagination, therefore, in the sense that we are using it, is the means by which we form *accurate* images of ourselves and our world. In this sense, it is the opposite of fantasy as popularly understood. In order for me to form such accurate images, I need a circle of friends, a nurturing community with whom I can continually test my vision. I need companions. Someone occasionally has to help me adjust my easel, to alter my perspective so that I can see a fresh landscape. I am continually prey to the inaccuracy of my images. The more stubbornly embedded I become in my own point of view, the more inaccurate my view of reality is.

The Christian promise of salvation inevitably brings me into conflict with myself because Christ offers me an image of who I essentially am. This true image reveals itself when I accept the fact that I am loved. There is spiritual combat between the self I am in practice and the self I am called to be. Christ invites me to wrestle with my own character. Indeed, one of the most arresting of the biblical images is Jacob wrestling with the angel in Genesis 32:24–31:

And Jacob was left alone; and a man wrestled with him until the breaking of the day. When the man saw that he did not prevail against Jacob, he touched the hollow of his thigh; and Jacob's thigh was put out of joint as he wrestled with him. Then he said, "Let me go, for the day is breaking." But Jacob said, "I will not let you go, unless you bless me." And he said to him, "What is your name?" And he said, "Jacob." Then he said, "Your name shall no more be called Jacob, but Israel, for you have striven with God and with men, and have prevailed." Then Jacob asked him, "Tell me, I pray, your name." But he said, "Why is it that you ask my name?" And there he blessed him. So Jacob called the name of the place Peniel, saying, "For I have seen God face to face, and yet my life is preserved." The sun rose upon him as he passed Peniel, limping because of his thigh.

Genesis 32: 24–31

Jacob receives a blessing and a new name (a new way of imaging and understanding himself and his destiny) but he is wounded in the encounter and leaves the place limping. Jacob had to wrestle with who he was and who he was becoming. The wonderful thing was that in the struggle, and only in the struggle, did Jacob begin to understand himself and his vocation. This passage of scripture speaks directly to me of Christian companionship which is characterized by a rhythm of wounding and blessing.

Jacob did his own struggling, and out of his wrestling came a new image of himself. This is the way of creative struggle with images. Images are destructive when they are forced upon us by society as socially useful or acceptable. Jacob, however, was a match for the angel of God who wrestled with him. His new understanding of himself was not forced upon him from outside, but came from within. Unless the new understanding is allowed to form us from within, it becomes restrictive and demoralizing. When who we are and who we are becoming is imposed on us from outside we are no longer free. Children often suffer because of the images parents force upon them. A father, for example, can easily use a son to live out many of the unrealized selves the older man harbors within himself. In such a situation the boy is unable to live from his own unique imagination, but is forced, for a while, to live out of his father's. The boy feels trapped because he has become a victim of his father's imagination. Part of the painful process of growing up will be his realization that he is not a victim after all. He is not a victim because he, like his father, also has an imagination.

But the question of images raises a deeper issue. How do we judge between the different and often disparate images which we have of ourselves and our world? Images are not of equal value. Many of them are destructive. What makes a particular image authentic? What is the nature of the authority of images? After all, we live in a supermarket of the imagination. So many options are open to us that we can put on a new "character" almost overnight. It might not go very deep, but our culture provides a multitude of costumes for a whole cast of characters. I express one or the other of this inner cast by the way I dress and behave. The wardrobes of the affluent are little more than a collection of costumes for various roles. "What shall I wear today?" disguises the question, "Who am I, really?" This is why theology is very important, because theology is concerned with the way we answer that basic question, "Who am I, really?", and with the ways in which we determine the authority of the images in the light of our answer. If, for example, my answer to the question, "Who am I?" is "I am a person of no consequence. Nobody cares about me and I don't give a damn!", I will understand myself and my world in a way which will best correspond to my basic image of myself and, of course, I will behave accordingly. If, on the other hand, I claim that "I am a child of God and the Temple of the Holy Spirit," I will respond to myself and the world in the light of that basic image. Even here we can be led astray. To see ourselves as the Temple of the Holy Spirit could lead us to embrace images which would fill us with self-importance. This is why spiritual guidance is important in our battle with the images. Even the good images can feed our self-deception.

Spiritual direction is an art, a creative process by which, together, we dare to imagine wild and exciting new possibilities for ourselves and for God's world. It is a dangerous business because it involves the transgression of limits and our entering into the unknown and unfamiliar. We can do and be far more than we know and it is often our lack of imagination that holds us back, keeps us tied down, and insists on our staying on the treadmill. It is very easy for us to see and feel what we are expected to see and feel simply because everybody else does. It took a small child who knew what he saw to cry out, "The Emperor has no clothes!" Everyone else "saw" them clearly enough. I have had many a spiritual companion who has been willing to play the role of that small child.

Spiritual direction is concerned with the creative use of the imagination to enable us to see what is really there. It requires the recovery of astonishment, and the revitalization of our withered imaginations. It means resisting the tendency to edit our experiences so that they will fit into everyone else's perspective. Children are our teachers in this respect. A three-year-old at play has not yet really developed the capacity to edit his experiences. He or she can turn a piece of wood into a horse or make a castle out of a cardboard box. It is fantasy to be sure, but it is creative fantasy because it is an imaginative process by which the child is introduced to an ever-increasing circle of possibilities.

Just as the child needs the nurturing and loving environment of a family (especially when he or she imagines a monster in the fold of a blanket or in the dark recesses of an open closet), so adults need a supportive community and a series of loving, nurturing relationships in order to negotiate the dark and threatening images that inevitably come to them. There is something wild, dark, and passionate within us, and the host of images that do battle inside us remind us that we are divided souls often torn inside by warring forces. We therefore need friends, fellow warriors. We also need an authoritative word from outside us which will give us a true image of ourselves.

The central issue is faith. Faith is our commitment to a key image by which the whole of reality is interpreted. For Christians, this interpretive key is a person, Jesus Christ. For some people, quite another key operates, and so inevitably there are warring views with regard to what is really real.

In William Golding's arresting novel *Darkness Visible*, for example, there is a dark and terrible character whose interpretive key is a kind of demonic alter ego inside her—a terrible thing without a name:

> Sometimes she wondered why nothing mattered and why she felt she could let her life trickle out of her hands if she wanted to, but most often she did not even wonder. The thing at the mouth

of her tunnel brandished a pretty girl who smiled and flirted and even sounded earnest now and then—"Yes I *do* see what you mean! We're destroying the world!" But the thing at the mouth of the tunnel said without sound—*as if I cared!*"[2]

Once our imagination becomes possessed of such an image it is hard to shake it off. We know people whose whole view of reality is jaundiced by an interpretive key that fosters a resentful, depressive, or even vengeful attitude. The key makes all the difference. A thick, unpolished, dirty lens seriously restricts one's view. We rarely see what is there simply because the organ of sight is defective or largely unused.

Consider a cat sitting in the sun. The novelist Walker Percy takes an ordinary cat and uses it to make us feel uneasy and uncomfortable with regard to our view of ourselves. Will Barrett, the hero of *The Second Coming*, contemplates a lazy cat sitting in the sun and gains a new vision of himself:

> As he sat gazing at the cat, he saw all at once what had gone wrong, wrong with people, with him, not with the cat—saw it with the smiling certitude with which Einstein is said to have hit upon his famous theory in the act of boarding a streetcar in Zurich.
>
> There was the cat. Sitting there in the sun with its needs satisfied, for where one place was the same as any other place as long as it was sunny . . . the cat was exactly a hundred percent cat, no more no less. As for Will Barrett, as for people nowadays—they were never a hundred percent themselves. They occupied a place uneasily more or less successfully. More likely they were forty-seven percent themselves, or rarely, as in the case of Einstein on the streetcar, three hundred percent. All too often these days they were two percent, spectators, who hardly occupied a place at all. How can the great suck of self ever hope to be a fat cat dozing in the sun?[3]

The sight of an ordinary house cat can excite deep questions and stimulate the imagination if one has eyes to see.

Spiritual direction is an art rooted in a deep appreciation of tradition and authority where the images are rich and varied. Richard Sennett in his book *Authority* answers the question, "Who is an authority?" by using the example of the great orchestral

conductor Pierre Monteux. This musician was no flamboyant show-
man. There was no coercion or threat in his manner of conducting,
but he was someone who had the power to stimulate the imagination by showing it a broader vision and by summoning it to a higher
allegiance: "He had the strength to see through you, to refuse what
your peers accepted. It made you anxious and kept you on your
toes."[4] A true spiritual authority challenges us with our own potential, our own vision, our own promise of glory. A true spiritual
authority leaves us busy thinking our own thoughts rather than
merely mouthing his. The one sure way to spot false authority in
spiritual matters is the suggestion that your troubles are over and
that you have arrived, that the work of your imagination is complete. A true spiritual authority leaves us with our own work to do.
There is no final ending.

We do not, therefore, want an authority who will do our imagining for us, but a person (or better, a fellowship of persons) who will
place us within an interpretive framework that will help us face our
own images creatively. Still less do we want to reject all authority
and go get lost in a private, often infantile world. Withdrawal into
the tiny world of ourselves might save us in the short term, but
without the stimulation of images from without we wither and die.
We want to be free, but we don't want to be alone.

To whom should I surrender? There are demagogues who invite
submission. There are ideologies which offer the interpretive key
to the meaning of life for which I long. Which way shall I turn?
Deeper into the dark recesses of the self? Or towards surrender to
the authority of another? The question remains. Who or what, in
the end, determines my picture of reality? The success of political
and spiritual totalitarianism in our age shows that many prefer
submission to external authority. One Stalinist journal proclaimed
in 1948: "The socialist regime liquidated the tragedy of loneliness
from which men of the capitalist world suffer."[5] Is that the choice
then? Totalitarianism or loneliness?

The Christian believes passionately in a third way. It is true that
it is a way of submission and obedience, but the object of such
self-abandonment is nothing less than God. Such self-abandonment
takes a lifetime because there are always lesser loves, minor allegiances, which demand our attention and obedience. Idolatry is still

rampant in the world and our battle is to be continually waged with the idols which threaten our primary allegiance. This fundamental commitment to God as our highest allegiance makes all other allegiances, however important, penultimate. Those who believe in the Christian gospel claim that their God is One whom "to serve is to reign" (or, as it is usually translated, "whose service is perfect freedom"). The Christian places his whole being in the hands of God and thus avails himself of the widest of all possible interpretive keys for his own self-understanding. It is, of course, not limitless in the sense that evil images are allowed to dominate (although they sometimes serve an important function). It is limitless, however, in the sense of the infinite creative possibilities for good which are daily opened up for us when we place ourselves in God's hands.

We should, however, never forget that images and metaphors can narrow as well as widen our view of ourselves. The metaphor can lie as well as tell the truth. Hitler often described the Jews as insects,[6] so that the word *Jew* stood for something small, crawling, and repulsive. Hitler did not have in mind gorgeous butterflies when he spoke of the Jews. Calling Jews "insects" or calling blacks "vermin" brutalizes both the name-caller as well as the ones thus vilified. It is no wonder that we fear those who can stir mobs to acts of violence. The spoken word can destroy as well as create, and a gifted demagogue can capture the imagination of a mob with a metaphor such as blacks are a disease or Jews an infection.

This brings us to another important function of the spiritual guide or friend. He or she can encourage a healthy skepticism in us with regard to the destructive images and metaphors we inevitably carry around in the attics and basements of our psyches. A friend of the soul will, at times, need to encourage us to *disbelieve* in some of the images we have of ourselves and of the world.

Michael Foucault in his *Discipline and Punishment* claims that "when one wishes to individualize the healthy, normal, and law-abiding adult, it is always by asking him how much of the child he has in him, what secret madness lies within him, what fundamental crime he had dreamt of committing."[7] This has startling implications for the vital role of spiritual direction in the formation of persons in community today. The environment set by the Holy Spirit allows our childishness/childlikeness, our madness (both creative and destructive), and our criminality (in both its daring and damaging aspects) to be given voice in an atmosphere that is both open and reverent. We need occasions (in confession or in spiritual direction) when we are permitted to share anything and everything within us without fear of rejection or condemnation. A good spiritual guide will enable the person seeking direction to sift through the images, rejecting some and responding to others. In other words, the spiritual guide offers strategical advice about the battles ahead. The two dominant metaphors which give shape to the battle within us concern images of freedom and of slavery. Are we lords or are we slaves? Lords over whom? Slaves of what?

Richard Sennett describes one philosopher's theory of authority in a way that helps us to view the spiritual director as a stimulator of the imagination:

> The stations of the journey are marked by crises of authority. Crises of authority are constructed around the modulations in recognizing freedom and slavery in oneself, recognizing them in other human beings. Each crisis occurs through disbelieving that one previously believed. But these acts of disbelieving are not ends. They are means to new patterns of belief. During the later phases of this churning over, when one recognizes with distress the Lord and servant within oneself, and then the Lord and servant within others, the upheavals alter the way one acts with other human beings. In the latter two phases, the old lord loses his power over the bondsman, not because the bondsman overthrows him or takes his place but because the unhappy bondsman becomes a different human being . . .[8]

A spiritual guide or friend is someone with whom it is both safe and constructive to disbelieve in order that a new pattern of believing may emerge. It is in such exchanges (sometimes threatening and frightening) that we are renewed, that we become different human beings. This process of disengagement from beliefs and the authority they have over us is very important at certain stages in spiritual growth. It enables us to pose the terrible but freeing question: "Are there other ways of looking at myself and my world?" Metaphors change, images shift, and a new picture of reality emerges. It often takes a crisis to radically change our way of looking at things. Sennett goes on:

Consciousness of lordship and bondage is all: crises change the
nature of a person's consciousness. More and more the ethics of
recognition—sympathy, sensitivity, modesty about oneself—should control the interpretation of power. This free recognition *is* freedom.
     It is an enormously idealistic, spiritual view, but anything but
a naive concept of liberty. Liberty is not happiness. It is an
experience of division, it is the final acknowledgment that a
tyrant and a slave live in every human being; only by acknowledging this fact can human beings ever hope to be more than
duelists.[9]

The image of the duel within is very ancient. Plato's well-known
image of the soul as a charioteer trying to control wild horses
springs to mind. But it is dangerously wrong to see the duel as one
between flesh and spirit. It is, rather, one between lord and slave.
It is a battle which is raging at the heart of Western civilization;
yet the lost art of spiritual direction proclaims that human beings
are much more than either duelists or dualists: duelists in the sense
of ultimately being divided and broken selves; dualist in the sense
of acknowledging a division between the flesh (understood as the
seat of evil) and spirit (understood as the throne of good). We are
invited to pay attention to *all* that we are, to be open to all life
offers. But living with true openness to the Holy Spirit is very
difficult because the freedom which such allegiance offers is unnerving. That is why religion has so often degenerated into a seductive kind of bondage. The freedom it offers is too much to bear.
Sennett poses the dark question at the root of our spiritual longings:
"How much exposure to uncertainty, to half measures, to unhappiness can humanity bear in order to be free?"[10]
     What is so maddening about the spiritual journey is that there
are so few footholds. What keeps us from falling? The Christian is
one who finds his whole life held both in being and in question by
a constellation of images (guarded and celebrated by a worshiping
community of fellow pilgrims) which enable him to face with
courage and hope the strange process of disbelieving in order to
believe more deeply. Without the courage to disbelieve we would
never move or grow. We tend to get set in our ways, embedded in
our point of view. The spiritual companion is one who, by stimulat-

ing our imagination and challenging us with the great Christian metaphor of death and resurrection (behind which is the Savior himself), can help us emerge from our state of embeddedness.

Closely allied with this false sense of the fixity of things ("nothing can or should change") is a sense that we are not actors in a drama, but rather acted upon. We are, in short, victims of circumstance: "It is out of my hands." We like to think of ourselves in this way. To be a victim is to be a slave to another's will, to the environment, to heredity, or to circumstances. Thus while we are unfree we are also (to our intense relief) not responsible. Our parents, our friends, our bosses—*they* are the ones who hurt us. Karl Marx's word for such people is the *Lumpenproletariat*—people who are victims of fate and for whom the emergence of the new is not a possibility. For them the system works and cannot be changed. The debilitating and demoralizing power of tyranny and oppression over the consciousness of men and women cannot be overemphasized. It is, of course, not only the poor and the oppressed who are the spiritual *Lumpenproletariat*—it is also the rich and the affluent.[11]

Spiritual direction (or better human life directed by the Holy Spirit) will not allow us the luxury of being members of the *Lumpenproletariat*, of being embedded in an unchanging view of reality, or of abandoning our responsibilities in the comforting role of victim. Religion at its worst (like its twin, politics) promises total security in exchange for total surrender. It is a terrible exchange, for, as we have insisted, the only proper object of our surrender is God. Religion often tries to claim for itself exclusive rights in the very name of the One to whom we are to surrender. Religion in this sense, however, bears as much resemblance to God as a photograph does to a lover.

I need healing images that will challenge my view of myself as either embedded or victimized. A spiritual guide can help me change the position of my easel and bring a whole new world into view. Maybe a friend of yours will invite you to take a good look at your cat busy being one hundred percent itself. Remember Will Barrett noticing his cat basking in the sun.

I am more and more conscious, as times goes on, that my life is held together by the kindness of friends, the casual remarks of strangers, the crazy and angry talk of my fellow citizens. Like Will

Barrett, I have "learned over the years that if you listen carefully you can hear the truth from the unlikeliest sources, especially from the unlikeliest sources, from an enemy, from a stranger, from children, from nuts, from overheard conversations, from stupid preachers . . ."[12] Yet are we willing and able to listen carefully, to pay attention to what is going on in and around us? Are we willing to allow our imagination to be activated and to face whatever we are given?

The great image with which the Christian is faced, both as a sign of judgment and of hope, is the Cross. It proclaims that liberty is not identical with happiness, and that there is no fulfillment without suffering. It also provides us with a power-bearing image which enables us to live through our sufferings and, in the grace of God, even make use of them. Suffering is sometimes a way out of "embeddedness." It reminds us of the terrible fragility of things. It undermines our faith in the permanence of existing arrangements. It weaves a vital link between freedom and limitation.[13]

Perhaps the worst suffering of all is the self suffering itself, the two-percent self sucking its own energy away. How am I to confront (without help, support, friends) "anxieties that seem to have neither name nor source, a strange exhilaration at the sufferings and tragedies that often people encounter, times of baseless dissatisfaction and boredom . . . a relish for hurting others, weird and malignant dreams, and a taste of ashes. There seems to be a maelstrom in the self somewhere, luring, tugging, insatiable."[14] I need friends, guides, a life-bearing tradition if I am to come through it all.

Carl Jung's criticism that Christianity often minimizes the strength of all the night creatures abroad in the self and set on its subversion is well founded. The idea that such things might be present in the committed Christian is abhorrent to many believers who claim that Christ's victory on the cross was so decisive that for the believer all is sweetness and light. Christ's victory was and is decisive, but the battle, though won, still rages. Christ not only suffers for us, but also in us and through us. "Jesus will be in agony until the end of the world," wrote Pascal, and this is a dark truth hard for Christians to swallow.

The battle, then, is a serious one and all the more insidious because we can easily fool ourselves into imagining that it is raging elsewhere. We need to cultivate an imagination for evil so that we can begin to see "our sucking two-percent self" for what it is. Only then can we join battle against the self which assumes that it is the center and measure of all things; against the self which is embedded, like a fly in amber, in our narrow interpretation of persons and events. Without the compelling power of creative if painful images we aid and abet one another in our false view of things. One has only to watch the television coverage of political conventions to see men and women willing to reinforce one another's view of the world. In self-defense we weave patterns of self-deception and so develop explanations by which we reject all that is not nice about us. Our imagination is so shriveled and narrow that we dare not admit that we are really as capable of evil as well as good. But then the reverse is also true. Many are consumed by self-hatred, self-disgust because they cannot imagine any other possibility, any other role for themselves.

The battle becomes particularly intense when we struggle with our own darkness and own it as ours. Spiritual guidance can provide us with an ever-widening interpretation of reality which will prevent us from being forced to lie to ourselves about our own evil and darkness. The good news of the gospel saves us from the necessity of self-deception. Christian maturity involves the growing ability to negotiate creatively an ever-widening range of experience in the company of others.

How do we dare battle? We dare because of the healing perennial experience of grace. We dare because underneath the darknesses and difficulties is the Holy Spirit guiding and sustaining all things. This is a statement of faith, but it is not a glib one, because the Christian faith commits the believer both to accepting judgment as well as to receiving forgiveness. Christian faith involves, on occasion, the embracing of an agony, the voyaging through shadows and threatening images. Spiritual direction is the process by which these images are transformed. A spiritual guide creates an environment in which the images can come to consciousness. The temptation is always to sink deeper and deeper into the unconscious and to surrender to its energies. Why? Because consciousness means an awareness of not only the good, the beautiful, and the true, but also of suffering, tragedy, and brokenness, and we need images, stories, sagas, and myths that are large enough to help us endure and in the end enjoy the truth.

In order, then, for us to make sense of the images that confront us we need an interpretive framework, a story, a gospel. The genius of evil is that it attacks the narrative thread which connects our life together. The gospel proclaims that our life does hang together and the scriptures and the Christian community provide the story that holds it all together.

My spiritual companion can help me imagine a future full of hope and promise without escaping the exigencies of the present or fantasizing from a cut-off base. He or she can help me do this because we are fellow pilgrims in a community which celebrates the enlarging images of the Cross and Resurrection: our two great antidotes to embeddedness and self-deception.

The imagination serves a critical function in our interpretation of the universe. Not only do images stretch and challenge our view of the world, they also provide us with the means by which we can challenge conventional and popular images in everyday life. Our view of reality will depend on the kind of questions we ask of it. Jacob Needleman writes:

> Imagine that a certain man comes upon a gun. He has never before seen or heard of such a thing. Nor, we must imagine, does he have any need to kill for food or defense. He picks up the gun, turns it around, knocks it against a stone. What is this object? He takes it home and experiments with it. To his delight he finds that when he holds it by the barrel he can crush things and break them better than with his wooden mallet. To him, the gun is a hammer. That is his idea, his theory, so to say, and his theory works. When others ask him what that strange object is, he can prove his answer through the test of experience.
> Why did this man not discover the proper nature of the gun?[15]

The man did not have a wide enough view of reality to include the real purpose of the gun. This is the way we are most of the time and it takes a sense of a larger reality to stretch our view of things. My problem is that I do not ask the right questions about life. I am like the man with the gun who uses it as a hammer. The questions I ask life are narrowly based and spring from petty and private concerns about survival and security. A friend of the soul brings me into a larger and more generous reality.

There are those places where the serious questions and the more powerful images invade my little world—in dreams, in the times when I am disciplined enough to keep a journal, and, above all, in my regular participation in a life of prayer (particularly as it is expressed liturgically). Dreams are full of unbidden images and unasked questions and are worthy of close attention. The keeping of a journal allows me the wonderful opportunity to think thoughts which would otherwise be suppressed. Prayer and worship open me up to an ever-widening world of questions and images.

The storehouse of Christian questions and images is, of course, the Bible. Indeed it is, with the liturgy, the supreme place where nourishment is to be found. The Old Testament is the story of men and women who heard God speaking to them, sometimes in dreams, often simply in their "inquiring of the Lord." It was a simple procedure. When you could not understand or bear what was happening in your life you went and asked God about it. This approach, for all its danger, is wonderfully direct and simple. And humanity loses a great deal when the sense of direct access to God is lost. The Elgoni, a tribe in East Africa, believed that God spoke to them and told them what to do through the dreams of their medicine men. When Jung visited them in 1925 they told him: "No, since the English came we have not had any more big dreams, for you see the District Commissioner knows what we should do."[16]

Barbara Hannah comments, "We all, whether we know it or not, more and more in these rational days trust the "District Commissioner" and all he stands for and have thus lost touch, for the most part completely forgotten, the superhumanly guidance that exists in the unconscious . . ."[17]

This is dangerous talk and many people have fallen into a whirlpool of madness because of it. Spiritual direction understands the danger, and for this reason spiritual growth always evolves within the context of a community that is firmly grounded in tradition. We need friends, guides, directors who will help us understand and interpret the questions and images, because deep questioning and the receiving of a wider vision of reality will mean nothing unless it overflows into everyday life and changes our patterns of behavior. It is no good if questions and images are trapped inside us and fail to bear fruit in the world.

Barbara Hannah, talking about the opportunities and dangers of the use of the imagination, writes:

> There is never any guarantee, if we once start on this path, as to where it may lead us. Above all, it should never be undertaken without a firm relationship to *someone* who will understand, or at least sympathize, for it sometimes leads into such cold and inhuman depths that *human companionship is absolutely necessary* to prevent us from getting entirely frozen and lost.[18]

The benefits, however, from being receptive to the images that come to us are incalculable. Images widen the range of our possibilities and our disciplined attention to that will be for "the enlarging of the heart." It should, however, be evident that the life of the imagination, whether it comes to us through our dreams, our journal keeping, or simply unbidden as we're walking down the street, is not to be taken lightly.

7

Spiritual Direction as a Work of Contemplation

The first imperative of all the great religions is "Be attentive!" and being attentive is what is meant by contemplation. Paying attention to what is simply there can involve a furious inner battle, especially when what is there threatens us. We explored earlier the battle human beings have with embeddedness, with their experience of being stuck in situations and relationships like butterflies or flowers encased in a paperweight. Being willing to pay close attention to what is there is the beginning of our being drawn out of that which traps and enslaves us. Without a companion I lack the courage to look reality squarely in the eye. Without a friend I am in danger of becoming frozen and lost.

The struggle begins when we find that there is a stubborn part of ourselves that does not wish to be rescued from its secure bed. Surely it is better to be secure and embedded than to be free and open? Who knows what might happen if I become unstuck? Ernest Becker in *The Denial of Death* accurately describes such a person.

> He holds onto the people who have enslaved him in a network of crushing obligations, belittling interaction, precisely because these people *are his shelter*, his strength, his protection against the world. Like most everyone else . . . [he] is a coward who will not stand alone on his own center, who cannot draw from within himself the necessary strength to face up to life. So he embeds himself in others.[1]

Actually, the self-diagnosis of people in this condition is, in part, correct. They cannot save themselves and they know it. The tragedy is that they don't realize that their very condition, if they could but see it clearly, leads to the freedom that only faith can bring. What the Christian faith urges us to do is to see—to pay attention to our real condition, to taste it and to live with it. When we begin to contemplate, to pay close attention to what is there, we cannot help but feel lost. We are out of our depth. We must come to the edge of things where we are invited to make "the leap of faith." The creator, for whom everything is possible, invites us to trust and to make the leap. In other words, the Christian is convinced that he or she has nothing to fear in paying attention to what *is*, no matter how dark and frightening. All my seeing, sooner or later, brings me to the threshold of faith. I realize that there are fathoms of water beneath me, and that I am lost. I also reach out in my need and discover that I am grasped by a joy and a love beyond my wild imaginings.

It is with this in mind that I want to examine our struggle to be more and more open, receptive, and available to reality. When I try to live more attentively, I am confronted by three realities that present themselves to me as monstrous threats, as things to be subdued and overcome. They are a sense of otherness, death, and necessity.

By the sense of otherness I simply mean the sheer intractability of other things and other people. Things and persons will not be organized, controlled, or manipulated by me. They will not accommodate themselves to me and fit in with the way in which I have organized my life. This "otherness" comes to me in the form of something trivial like a nail that refuses to go into the wood straight. Otherness confronts me at those times when I attempt to blame circumstances rather than myself. I say, for example, "I got on the wrong train" when, as Dorothy Sayers pointed out, there aren't any wrong trains, only wrong passengers. Otherness, however, confronts me most deeply in other people. When I first encounter another person as truly other (rather than as an appendage of myself) it can be truly wonderful and yet terrifying. It is very disturbing when I meet someone who will not fit neatly into my little world. My tendency then is to reject, dismiss, render "nothing" those who will not fit into my scheme of things. It is not difficult to see why I need companionship, if only to rub up against someone else as a separate being, as someone *other* than myself.

The problem of otherness confronts me most sharply in regard to God. Here is the One who is completely beyond my grasp, out of my hands, beyond my control. God comes to me supremely as the Other. And I am invited to wait for him in patience. I like company while I wait.

When I begin to pay attention to what *is*, I inevitably run into the reality of my own mortality. Life is truly mortifying. Nothing lasts, and I have daily reminders of the transitoriness of things. Things fall apart. The roof needs repairing, my hair turns gray, my legs give way. There's a warning murmur in the heart. Even situations do not last. Relationships move and grow (or decay). Yet out of the very transitoriness of my life new things emerge. It's as if death is necessary for the release of new energy. That is why death was often conceived of in sacrificial terms. It was the means by which life was made new. There is a very ancient idea that the stuff by which we live is released only in death, and this energy has to be produced either intentionally—as a conscious activity by people committed to a spiritual way of self-sacrifice—or unintentionally—by war, famine, disaster, or premature death. If there is any truth in this ancient idea, then the commitment to live life contemplatively, to pay close attention to what *is*, is a genuine and creative alternative and antidote to war and human conflict. The inner attentiveness with which we contemplate our own death, therefore, has an important contribution to the peace of the world. This is a belief very close to the heart of Christianity: that is, the creative love by which we live is released only by an act of self-emptying, by a sacrificial dying. Christians are invited to share in the victory of Christ's sacrificial death by which the world is saved. Contemplation, or paying attention to what is, is a way of entering the mystery.

The classic name for paying close attention to our dying is *mortification*. The idea is not as morbid as it sounds. It was used only as a means to an end and not an end in itself. The purpose of "acts of mortification" was to place the Christian in a state of wider openness to God. The Christian was able to regard the irritating inconveniences and general vicissitudes of life as reminders of the bigger questions and the wider vision. Death is a salutory reminder that we are not to be the center of our attention. Dom Augustine

Baker in his *Holy Wisdom* says that we need to be reminded constantly of the centrality of faith in God and that life's mortifications save us from being eccentric (off center): "Naturally we love and seek nothing but ourselves in all things, whatsoever we love and seek. We are our own last end, referring all things, even supernatural—yea, God Himself—to our own interest—to our own interest and commodity." Mortification (the facing of death in the things of life) is, therefore, to give us both clearsightedness and discernment with regard to the things that really matter.

The seeing of things as they really are involves a constant confrontation with necessity which, of course, is intimately connected with the other two obstacles to our peace of mind: otherness and death. Here we are faced with the sheer intractability of existence. Many of us simply want to renegotiate existing arrangements and construct a world to our own specifications. All three obstacles require the miracle of love by which they are not so much overcome as transfigured. In one form or another confrontation with these three is the basic stuff of the spiritual journey. Our willingness to face (and our subsequent resistances to) the three constitute the warfare of which we have been speaking. We should not—and need not—face them alone.

Paying attention sounds simple, "as easy as falling off a log." It seems a bit far-fetched to use the metaphor of battle when dealing with what should be the simplest and most tranquil of activities. We associate contemplation, quite rightly, with stillness and peaceful centeredness.

Contemplation is simple attentiveness to what is there. But what is *there*? For the Christian, contemplation is based on an act of faith that what is really there will reveal itself. But what is really there remains unseen, hidden to the casual or lazy eye. Much of our "seeing" is merely scanning the surface of things, taking in the superficialities. Quiet attention takes great patience in waiting for what is truly there to manifest itself. Contemplation requires the focused and patient attentiveness of the bird-watcher (to use Archbishop Anthony Bloom's metaphor). This waiting for the other to manifest itself is difficult. It takes a long time for me to see the moth or the lizard which easily blends in with its own environment for protection. What I first took for a broken twig or a dried leaf turns out, to my surprise, to be a living thing. My battle is in the waiting, for I find it very hard to take seriously the reality of other things. I have little respect or reverence for their being, their sovereignty. I am like a child, believing that reality is simply an extension of myself.

Year after year in the spring the countryside where we live is infested with gypsy moths. This year there is not a leaf left on either the large maple or the copper beech. The caterpillars must be trapped and killed if the trees are to survive another year. My four-year-old son sees me killing them and joins in. I am struck by the fact that he, as yet, doesn't realize that they are separate living things which we regretfully destroy in order to save the trees. I realize that one of my tasks as a parent is to teach my son respect for the otherness of creatures. He knows already that sometimes reality bites or burns, making its otherness felt. It is at such moments that he begins to take it seriously. He has learned to respect the bright flickering flames of the fire, and the wild attractiveness of the waves pounding on the beach. They have already revealed their otherness to him in a powerful way. Much of our learning as children is involved in respecting and appreciating the world outside ourselves. We find that reality bites back when it isn't respected.

This battle for the recognition of otherness goes on into adult life in more subtle forms. Our tendency, psychologically, is to absorb everything that we see and that happens to us and to make it part of *our* world. Christian contemplation is our refusal to do that. It is a painful exercise in seeing that the real world is not one over which we have control. Contemplation is a response to a call from within us to go beyond ourselves, beyond our little world, and to relate freely to what is beyond us, outside our control. It is in such relationships that we are stretched beyond our limits. When we reach out to the other as other our little view of things has to be broken open. When I relate freely and in love to another person (and respect his or her otherness as something distinct and separate from me) anything can happen, because I have, for a while, given up my right to control and monitor reality.

I would like to create this other out of my own self, but, of course, I cannot. If I could do that it wouldn't be truly other. It would merely be something I had made up. Much of what passes for human love relies on such a device. I create my perfect beloved out of my own hopes and fantasies and am hurt and disappointed when he or she is disappointingly other. Love on my own terms becomes embittering and disappointing when the beloved does not live up to the specifications laid down by the lover. Without an other, however, I may be in charge of my own little world, I may be supreme sovereign of my little island, but I am, nevertheless, alone. When I am utterly alone I become anxious and bored, so I risk opening myself to the other. Quite simply, at first, I open myself up to *see* rocks, trees, clouds, and birds as separate and other. My world becomes an open world and, in some sense, ceases to be mine alone.

Perhaps we can now admit that contemplation—paying attention to reality—is something of a battle? Contemplation is very humbling because it is not an activity in which I do anything, least of all transcend myself by my own efforts. That would be like pulling myself up by my own shoelaces. Contemplation, rather, is an act through which I myself an transcended. It involves a humbling act of surrender wherein I give up my efforts to drag everything into the tight little orbit of my personal world. It involves the admission that there are some things or, better, that there is "Something" or "Someone" I am unable to capture in my spiritual butterfly net.[2]

It is very unnerving to admit that there are vast expanses of reality that are thus uncapturable and (in case we get too smug and claim that reality to us is a "mystery" and that we are indeed patient and reverent towards all creation) we need to be reminded that there is no greater butterfly net than religion itself. Religious people are often seduced into believing that they have a respect for others as other when all they have done is to suck all into their own little view of what constitutes mystery or religion.

The battle to contemplate helps to prevent our capturing other people for their own good. The recalcitrant and difficult other puts an enormous question to me about the way I have ordered my little kingdom. People are truly other from me. You, my companion and friend, are not, after all, merely something. Something is always an identifiable part of my world. You are other, and insofar as you are other you are like God—present, but hidden. In that hiddenness lies the promise of true intimacy, true because it is beyond manipulation or projection.

How does the other manifest itself? Often I catch a sense of the genuine other when I feel a terrible absence in my life. It's as if I had lost or mislaid something. Sometimes I am overcome by a sense of nostalgia, a deep longing for something I once had but no longer possess. The other, then, manifests itself to me and in me as something missing, or as some place to which I long to return. I am like Mr. Kips in Graham Greene's novel *Dr. Fischer of Geneva.* I am bent double, walking around looking for something I have lost. Contemplation at such times as these is a deep kind of longing.

At other moments I am rebellious and fearful. I sense an otherness within me which I want to reject or even destroy. I must tear it from me because it makes me unhappy about myself. The other then comes to me not only as something I have lost or mislaid, but also as something that must be exiled. It makes claims on me. It probes. It judges. In an earlier generation it might have been called conscience. All I know is that there is something or someone other than myself which lays claim on me. It demands that I give up my sovereignty over my little world. In the words of Richard Norris, the other is not "the silent mystery of our being but a word outside which calls, measures, condemns, reveals and reconciles." Contemplation under such circumstances is penitential. Paying close attention to reality produces in me a deep kind of sorrow because it shows me up for what I am. It shows up just how wrongheaded my plans for my self-realization are. I want no word from *outside*, nothing that is truly *other*, telling me about myself, challenging me, measuring me, and condemning me. Why, then, do I pay attention to it? Because this word from outside, often spoken by a friend, also heals and reconciles.

Finally, there is an other deep inside me which longs to respond to the word that comes to me from outside. I often know it is there by the enormous effort that is required to silence it. This other has been called "the still small voice": the internal testimony of the Holy Spirit.

The other who is God seeks an intimate relation with us. He comes to us as an other for whom we long, as an other who confronts

us with our true selves and reconciles us to ourselves, as an other
who is present in the deepest part of ourselves. Christians identify
this other as God, the Holy and undivided Trinity: Father, Son, and
Holy Spirit. The dogma of the Trinity is a way of pointing out how
the other comes home to us both in love and in judgment. Our
relationship to God is marked by both battle and peace, or as
Brother Roger of Taizé puts it, "struggle and contemplation."

Christian contemplation is paying loving attention to God, the
Blessed Trinity. It is a supremely creative act because when we do
this the other ceases to be a nagging question, but becomes a
healing and pervasive presence. There is a fantastic sense of liberty
when we are so attentive as to find ourselves in a center outside
ourselves. The otherness of God comes to us in three liberating
modes: as a return to our ground and source (God, the Father); as
a response in obedience to a Word (God, the Son); as a listening to
the spirit within us (God, the Holy Spirit).

Richard Norris writes:

> [Prayer is] a situation in which a person is *con-centrated* upon,
> pulled together in utter attentiveness to, the "other"; that is to the
> ground in which his being is contained, to the Word in which his
> being is addressed to him, and to the Spirit in which his being
> is interiorly actualized.[3]

We are not the center of our attention and it is often a struggle to
get us to realize this simple fact.

Strangely, when I am not concentrated on myself and on my
petty schemes things begin to happen in me. Indeed *I* begin to
happen. When I am focused outside myself the "I" I thought I was
explodes and a wider and more generous I emerges. When I am not
thus concentrated on something other than myself I am left with
the taste of me in my mouth which after awhile becomes sour and
bitter.

One of the infuriating things about the God who is revealed as
other is that he will not be manipulated. I cannot trap him in my
butterfly net by some spiritual technique or religious technology.
Using the word spirituality in a pejorative fashion, Richard Norris
concludes his paper on *Hunting the Transcendent* by contrasting
spirituality with mysticism. The former is a form of religious tech-

nology, the latter is the free surrender in love to the other who is God. "The nice thing about spirituality is that it allows us adventure while giving us the assurance that we remain firmly in our own hands. The inconvenience of mysticism . . . is that it leaves us in the hands of the other, that it keeps us eternally on pilgrimage."

The implications of this analysis for spiritual direction are enormous. The friend of my soul keeps the other constantly in focus. Indeed, he or she is the sign of the otherness which I need if I am to be released from the cell of my own sweating self. A spiritual companion will not allow me to be seduced by technology which will help me control the spiritual, but will always hold out to me the challenge and promise of surrender.

Seeing what is really there in life means seeing darkness and death all around us. That may not be all there is, but death is always present and much of our energy is spent in denying the obvious. No wonder we resist the call to be more contemplative. Paradoxically, a commitment to a life of attentiveness relies on a willingness to wait in the darkness until the other reveals itself. The truth sometimes takes a long unveiling and it takes patience to wait in the darkness, to allow our eyes to adjust to it, to allow God to reach us.

There are two opposing traditional views of darkness. The first is that darkness or night is the source of all evil. It is a time when demons and monsters of the deep roam the earth. Night is a time for vigilance, for preparing for battle. The second view, however, insists that night is the time for lovers. It is a sign of the depth of love, of a different kind of light. St. John of the Cross combined both ideas in his "dark night" which begins in struggle and torment and ends in the ecstasy of love. In the end the light and the love of God are encountered in the darkness.[4]

Much of what is said about the life of prayer can be applied to the dark world of our dreams. Dreams and prayer reveal a disquieting fact about human beings. They show us that we are plural and not singular, that we are many selves and not just one. When we dream or when we surrender ourselves in prayer we find, then, that we are many selves; the Christian is the one who seeks to be concentrated on God rather than on the chimera of his many selves. It is only in God that I find myself, or rather, I am found in him. When

I concentrate on myself I discover that I am legion. That is why I experience God first as savior, saving me not so much from one shriveled self, but from my many conflicted selves.

Not only does contemplation, like dreams, reveal my plurality and need for a savior, it also uncovers my vulnerability, my fragility, by placing me on the threshold of death. Contemplation invites me to wait in the darkness without the comforting array of familiar images which half fill my play pen. It puts a great distance between me and my image of myself by placing me on the edge of death. Death, as the hidden metaphor of the spiritual life, is the source of its energy and power. Unless we face this we are condemned to a deadly way of living: deadly because all our energy will be spent suppressing the truth about death. It is a strange fact that the more we are open to and aware of death the more we are alive to the present and each moment.

Facing the reality of death sounds like strange advice, but unless we do, religion, like psychiatry, can be caricatured as a disease masquerading as a cure. Religion becomes a hollow and, in the end, cruel exercise in sentimentality. Unless death is faced, neither can it be overcome. There is no victory, no triumph, no joy.

Contemplation, then, places me on the threshold of death, in the Halls of Hades. Why? To break open my little world and my narrow way of looking at things. In my willingness to wait in the darkness comes new possibilities. "In patience is your soul" is an ancient religious maxim which finds an echo in Luke 21:19, which can be translated: "In patience you will possess your soul," or as it has also been translated, "In patience you will find your true face."

The key word in contemplation is *patience*, which means to suffer, to endure, as well as to wait. It is patience which gathers all things together in the end. There is no true attentiveness to reality without the endurance of some kind of suffering. As James Hillman eloquently writes: "the soul is found in the reception of its suffering, in the attendance upon it, the waiting it through. From the soul's point of view, there is little difference between *patient* and *therapist*. Both words in their roots refer to attentive devotion, waiting on and waiting for."[5] This insight can be directly applied to the relationship fostered in spiritual direction and the various ways in which we can be a healing presence to and for one another. In spiritual direction both the director and the one seeking direction wait on and wait for God. They also wait on and for one another. The basic metaphor of spiritual direction, like that of therapy, is death; except that, in the case of spiritual direction, it is death seen in the context of the saving death of Christ. That is what makes it bearable. That is what makes it a triumph. In a way nothing matters more than death (as Ernest Becker has eloquently argued in his *Denial of Death*) in the sense that it is this which places all our questionings and hoping in the context of the saving death of Christ.

The contemplation of death helps me see mere spiritual technology for what it is: the cosmetic surgery performed on a corpse. I try to live by faith and not by technique. Paying close attention to my mortality prevents me from using contemplation for my own purposes, my own schemes, so that I can add it to my list of accomplishments. In fact, contemplation is liberating precisely because it is not *for* anything. It is, in terms of this world, nonproductive. It is for its own sake. It is an act of love. As such it is not to be regarded as a performance, something we *do* in order to be rewarded. Yet it is a work. Our daily encounter with our death and with our dying is a cosmic act in cooperation with the One who is revealed in Christ as a self-denying center, and it is in the power of God, the Blessed Trinity, that our death is transfigured into the energy by which we live.

Part of the task of spiritual direction is to identify those elements in human life which are the bearers of deadliness. Death comes in many guises and needs to be unmasked before it can come to us as a true metaphor of life, as the ultimate metaphor of the surrendered and, therefore, free life. Teilhard de Chardin[6] calls death the final moment of ex-centration; the moment when we are truly concentrated upon God. Meanwhile, we are a long way from our not being the center of our own attention! Our mortification is a long process by which false images of death are done to death.

> So, gradually, the worker no longer belongs to himself. Little by little, the great breath of the universe has insinuated itself into him through the fissure of his humble but faithful action, has broadened him, raised him up, borne him on.[7]

This is, in large part, true, although there is also the struggle and the pain of realizing that we do not belong to ourselves but to Another. Part of our struggle is *against* death and not a submission to it. Death must be embraced naked and unadorned, for death in disguise is not the liberating death of the Christian hope, but the living death of those who submit to a slow poison which deadens but never kills. Walker Percy in *The Second Coming* meticulously identifies this deadliness that does not bring true death, but a death-in-life.

> Death in the guise of Christianity is not going to prevail over me. If Christ brought life, why do the churches smell of death?
> Death in the guise of God and America and the happy life of home and family and friends is not going to prevail over me . . .
> Death in the guise of belief is not going to prevail over me, for believers now believe anything and everything and do not love the truth, are in fact in despair of the truth, and that is death.
> Death in the guise of unbelief is not going to prevail over me, for unbelievers believe nothing, not because truth does not exist but because they have already chosen not to believe, and would not believe, cannot believe, even if the living truth stood before them, and that is death.
> Death in the form of isms and asms shall not prevail over me, orgasms, enthusiasm, liberalism, conservatism, Communism, Buddhism, Americanism, for an ism is only another way of despairing of the truth.
> Death in the guise of marriage and family and children is not going to prevail over me. What happened to marriage and family that it should have become a travail and a sadness, marriage till death do us part yes but long dead before the parting, home and fireside and kiddies such a travail and a deadliness as to make a man run out into the night with his hands over his head? Show me that Norman Rockwell picture of the American family at Thanksgiving dinner and I'll show you the first faint outline of the death's-head.
> God may be good, family and marriage and children and home may be good, grandma and grandpa may act wise, the Thanksgiving table may be groaning with God's goodness and bounty, all the folks healthy and happy, but something is missing. What is this sadness here? Why do the folks put up with it? The truth seeker does not. Instead of joining hands with the folks and bowing his head in prayer, the truth seeker sits in an empty chair as invisible as Banquo's ghost, yelling at the top of his voice:

*Where is it? What is missing? Where did it go? I won't have
it! I won't have it! Why this sadness here? Don't stand for it!
Get up! Leave! Go live in a cave until you've found the thief
who is robbing you. But at least protest. Stop, thief! What is
missing? God? Find him!*[8]

There is very little we need to add about facing the givens of life.
Death and otherness are the twin necessities with which we have
to do battle. W. H. Auden writes to his godson, Philip Spender:
"Thank God your being is unnecessary!" Which is another way of
saying "Thank God you're not God!" Spiritual maturity, often
gained only through hard struggle, "is the growing realization that
there is no necessity in us except indeed that of being united with
the primal and only Necessity [God]. . . . The only illusion is that
here is in us a necessity to demand something other than He; the
only disillusion is to find that it is not so and that our only necessity
is love."[9]

How can we live with only one necessity, that is, the love of God?
Most of us relate to one another out of necessity, and it is this which
mars all our loving. Love requires freedom. Necessity is the enemy
of freedom, and yet strangely in this world it is also its ground and
condition, provided we can tell the difference between what is truly
necessary and what isn't. Simone Weil writes: "When the attachment of one being to another is made up of needs and nothing else
it is a fearful thing. Few things in this world can reach such a depth
of ugliness and horror. There is always something horrible whenever a human being seeks what is good and only finds necessity."[10]

She goes on to affirm that the only way human beings can relate
to one another creatively is through love and true love requires a
miracle, an act of God. That miracle is friendship, and friendship
is a state where two people have consented to remain two (that is,
they reverence and honor one another's otherness; they respect the
distance between them) and are united to each other not directly
but indirectly in God. Only He is large enough to hold them together and, at the same time, maintain the distance between them
which true friendship requires. "Pure friendship is an image of the
original and perfect friendship that belongs to the Trinity and is the
very essence of God. It is impossible for two human beings to be

one while scrupulously respecting the distance that separates them, unless God is present in each of them."[11] There we have a definition of Christian companionship. It is that state of union in which difference and distance are as respected and honored as holding and binding. To be a companion, in this sense, is to be stretched out on the cross of life. To be open and vulnerable to another and, at the same time, to reverence and respect his or her otherness is part of what it means to enter a little into the mystery of the Passion of Christ. It is the passion, God's passion, to which we must finally turn our full attention.

8

Christian Companionship Is Joy in Sacrifice

Who am I? My deepest realization of who I am
is that I am one loved by Christ.
Thomas Merton

There is no way that the Christian can escape the call to sacrifice. It is central to his or her interpretation of reality.
Indeed human creativity and the hope for fulfillment presuppose
it. The creation of the simplest thing requires sacrifice because, in
order to create, something has to be given up: time, energy, and
alternative possibilities. The creative artist has to make everything
he does serve his artistic vision. Creativity, then, requires sacrificial
singlemindedness.

Meaningful existence presupposes another kind of surrender: a
willingness to be broken open for the sake of growth. Our primal
impulse is to transcend ourselves, and that impulse (what the mystics call the *extensio animi ad magna*, the stretching of the soul to
great things) is fundamentally sacrificial. It stretches the human
spirit to the breaking point and beyond; yet without that impulse
toward great things human life degenerates into mediocrity and
triviality. I hardly know what I'm doing sometimes and I can easily
lapse into the blind and casual indifference characteristic of our
age. Spiritual direction challenges that indifference and opens me
to the demands and fulfillment of the sacrificial and creative way
of Christ. The director or friend of the soul presents us with the way
of the Cross, which in the power of the Spirit becomes a "royal
way" to our deepest joy.

The concept of sacrifice is rich, vague, and varied. It covers anything from God's outpouring of himself in creation to a human being's giving up something good in order to gain something better. But the notion of sacrifice has suffered a serious eclipse, especially in the West since the end of the Second World War. The concept has been discredited with apparently the best of motives. It was often closely linked with patterns of self-rejection and with psychological and spiritual self-flagellation which characterized some forms of religious observance.

The attack on the call to sacrifice has been impressive: First it can be argued that the insistence of the centrality of sacrifice is repressive and neurotic, that it hampers the development of human potential, and in many cases actually causes what appears to be permanent psychic deformity.

There is some truth in this attack on sacrificial living. We know too much about depth psychology to be seduced by the subtle manipulations of those who have surrendered themselves to a cause, to a disciplined life, or even to a dying parent. We are all too familiar with the person who has surrendered himself to his work in what amounts to a self-destructive frenzy. These objections are not directed at the idea of sacrifice as such, but at false or inadequate objects of sacrifice. This raises the theological question we have asked in several places in the preceding chapters: What is the appropriate object of sacrifice? of surrender? Let me say again: Human life is meaningless without some sort of sacrifice at its heart, and spiritual direction is meant uncompromisingly to point to God as its only object.

Second, there is the objection that the notion of sacrifice is spiritually unhealthy: Sacrifice, it is argued, not only hinders or damages us psychologically, but it also hinders our approach to God. The argument continues that it may have been appropriate in an earlier age, but we do not honor God today by self-abandonment, by fear, or by repentance. The age of mortification is over and good riddance! It is further argued that growth in spiritual freedom is commensurate with the individual's capacity to grow out of a dependence on a higher reality and to stand on his own two feet. The real secret of Christianity, it is said, is self-fulfillment, not self-abandonment.

Again, there is some truth in this line of argument. The sacrificial life can be spiritually destructive, can feed on our own masochistic tendencies. To leave the matter there, however, would be to surrender spirituality to a very limited psychology that seduces us into accepting a wildly reductionist view of ourselves. There is often little room for aspiration and no room for sacrifice. "Leave me alone. This is the way *I am.*" There is no stretching of the soul after great things. Our age is characterized by both shallow patterns of self-rejection and self-acceptance. In both cases the self is as dry and shriveled as a prune.

Our reactions to this sad state of affairs can range from the cultivated cynicism of the lapsed or lapsing liberal to the tight little pieties of frustrated and disappointed conservatives. There are, of course, other energies at work—energies of compassion, energies of love, energies of the Holy Spirit. It is, in the end, the energy of grace that saves us from both our high idealism (with all its ego-investment) and our low self-image (with its even more intense ego-investment). Grace restores in us the idealism of the Spirit, and spiritual direction fosters our rootedness in God and in the world he has made.

In order to accept and proclaim the Christian hope in all its fullness and in all its joy, we have to rediscover the road of sacrifice and accept the two great and traditional dissuasives to Christian discipleship: darkness and suffering. But I don't want to stop there and have all of us wallowing in negativity and self-rejection. The sacrificial life is also the liberated and the liberating life. The Christian life leads neither to self-fulfillment nor self-rejection, but to self-transcendence. It is for the enlarging of the heart. It is for love. It is for delight. And the relationship I have with a spiritual director serves to widen more and more my capacity not only to face darkness and suffering but also to stretch the mind and heart to bear love and delight.

If the element of sacrifice is central to human life, and further, if we Christians understand that sacrifice is expressive of the very nature of God, then it must permeate the whole created order. Sacrifice molds and makes the world. That is why humanity is priestly; the priest is, by definition, one who offers sacrifice. Each one of us needs to recover his or her priestly identity in Christ. We are people of sacrifice because sacrifice lies in the heart of God. It is creative rather than destructive. It is for the release of new life, for the liberation of energy. Sacrifice is, therefore, creative, nurturing, and transforming. And, in this sense, the relationship we have in spiritual direction is sacrificial.

Our road to this rediscovery, however, is a long one. So much of what we thought humanity was has to be discarded. There is an irreducible *uselessness* about human life no matter how successful we are or how many skills we acquire. We Christians are *useless* in the sense that we do not find our identity in what we do but in who we are. "Who am I? My deepest realization of who I am is that I am one loved by Christ." This means that I am always found in the ever-widening context of Christ's love. We are signs of transcendence, we are more than we will ever know. At the same time we are signs of death. Christians stand as a reminder to people of unfinished business, of the fact that status does not confer identity. To live with no tight, neat role is truly sacrificial. It is also truly creative because it leaves us open and free (dare we say) like God himself.

Let us go back to that primordial sacrificial act by which God created the universe. In Raimundo Panikkar's monumental work, *The Vedic Experience,* he points out that in the earliest Hindu scriptures there are three essential "moments" in the unfolding of reality: solitude, sacrifice, and integration. (Here I am deliberately choosing to use the insights of a religious tradition other than our own to uncover the vast treasurehouse of Christian insight which we have sorely neglected.)

Solitude is the first "moment" and is the inevitable concomitant of self-awareness. When we are given a new vision of ourselves and of the world, we are pushed deeper and deeper into solitude. Perhaps that is why so many of us are resistant to spiritual growth? The threat of solitude frightens us. Carl Jung wrote in his early letters:

> The journey from cloud-cuckoo-land back to reality lasted a long time. In my case Pilgrim's Progress consisted in my having to climb down a thousand ladders until I could reach out my hand to the little clod of earth that I am. . . . Shouldn't we rather let God himself speak in spite of our only too comprehensible fear of the primordial existence? I consider it my task and duty to educate my patients and pupils to the point where they can

accept the direct demand that is made upon them from within. The path is so difficult that I cannot see how the indispensable suffering along the way could be supplanted by any kind of technical procedure. Through my study of early Christian writings I have gained a deep and indelible impression of how dreadfully serious an experience of God is. It will be no different today.[1]

The dreadful seriousness of the experience of God first brings loneliness and fear, what the evangelical tradition calls "conviction of sin."

The very act of creation is sacrificial. The reaching out which every creative act requires is a breaking open of the self. Without the breaking open of the self there is no delight! How can there be if the self is trapped inside itself? Sacrifice is exposure. It is vulnerability. This is what drives us. This is the energy that makes us tick.

This might not be the language we would normally use, but it surely has its analogue in the Christian tradition. It is enshrined for us in the doctrine that each one of us is made after the image of God. It is celebrated in the great feast of the Ascension. Our destiny is in God. Our destiny (in Christ) is glory, which is being in all its fullness.

Traditionally, a sacrifice was the center of a dynamic process in which the divine and the human came into contact. In the Hebrew tradition it was the seal of a covenant, the sign of a love affair, the mark of delight. For Christians the sacrifice of Christ on the cross showed that in Jesus the divine and the human come into contact in such a way that they can never be parted. It did more than show. It effected what it revealed.

In both Hebrew and Greek traditions the notion of sacrifice does not suggest reluctance, sadness, or deprivation, but rather their opposites: joy, festivity, and thanksgiving. The emphasis is on the giving and not so much on the giving up. There are five elements:

1. the *gift* of the human being to the deity in which the gift and the giver become identified one with the other;
2. the *homage* of subject to Lord;
3. the *expiation* of offenses;
4. *communion* with the deity;
5. *life* released from the victim.

These five marks are characteristic not only of the Christian life itself, but also of the relationships we have within the Church which stretch and nurture us. Spiritual direction is an act of worship, an act of self-giving to God in which there is an inevitable coming together of both penitence and joy in the celebration of and delight in new life. Our sacrificial relationship to God requires self-offering and adoration. Because sacrifice seals a relationship of love it is characterized by absolute honesty. There is, therefore, penitence and forgiveness. Above all, there is communion and the release of power which gives life.[2] Sacrifice, in this sense, characterizes Christian companionship.

Sacrifice is our response to the deepest longings within us. It speaks to our desire to be possessed, to be stretched beyond our limits, to transcend ourselves. Indeed it is so powerful that it can lead to tragedy and death, like the literal flaming zeal of those persons in recent memory whose impulse to sacrifice was so strong that they actually set fire to themselves. However we interpret such extreme action, it does point to a deep and dangerous impulse. We do desire to be possessed, taken up, engulfed; but if we are possessed, taken up, or engulfed by anything less than God, tragedy and destruction ensue. This is why I need a friend of the soul to keep me on course.

Perhaps the greatest sacrifice of all that we in the West have to make is our conceptual control of things, especially our conceptual manipulation of the Christian religion in general and of the person of Christ in particular. Ray Bradbury has written the outline of a science fiction story which illustrates the terrible controlling power of the mind and imagination.

> Late at night on Mars, two priests speak of their reasons for joining the Church. The younger priest confesses that "I joined hoping one day to actually *meet* Christ should he truly return."
> The priests retire to sleep. At three in the deep morning, the young priest stirs, wakens, listens to the Martian wind grieve about the small colonial church. He hears a steady dripping sound from below, in the baptistry. Moving silently, he peers into the dark baptismal room and cries out!
> Just beyond the font, self-illuminated, stands the figure of a white-robed man, bearded, with fiery eyes.
> The dripping sound? It is caused by the upraised hand of the

Man from whose palm slow drops of blood fall into the baptismal waters.

The priest, stunned, falls to his knees, calling out to this apparition, no, this reality: At last, oh, at last, after more than two thousand years, you've come!

No! the Apparition cries. Stand back, avert your gaze! I am not the Thing you imagine. I am not the Walker by the Sea of Galilee! Your thought will kill me. Turn away!

And in that moment the priest realizes that his childhood dream of someday meeting Christ has moved out into the Martian night and trapped a Martian. The Martians have telepathic abilities. They can assume the shapes of dreams, appear in any guise that the imagination summons forth. So *this* Martian, seized into the Church by the priest's dream, trapped by his hoping, desiring mind, appears as Christ.

Let go! the Martian pleads.[3]

What a terrible sacrifice it is for us to give up some cherished image of ourselves, of Christ, of God. The fact is that God offers us himself and not a system of ideas. The agony of our hoping, desiring mind as it waits in sacrificial silence is intense. There is a temptation to soften the pain by a facile reconciliation of differences, by a blind and stubborn refusal to bear paradox. We long for explanations. So the creeds, those magnificent metaphysical stutterings of the human intellect, degenerate into explanations of mysteries. Instead of pointing to mystery, the formulas themselves become objects of faith or of ridicule. It is absurd both to swallow the creeds as explanations or to attempt to update them in order to make them sound more plausible. Both the credal fundamentalist and the credal reformer make the same mistake in imagining that the creeds are explanations of mystery. The best form of the creed is the *Te Deum Laudamus*: "We *praise* thee O God," not we understand, comprehend, fathom you, O God. Entry into the divine mystery is through the door of adoration. Adoration keeps the doors of our grasping mind continually open. It also refreshes and cleanses our relationships.

On November 6, 1915, Carl Jung wrote a vitally important letter to his friend Hans Schmid, in which he speaks of the terrible dangers of imagining that we have finally understood anything.

... the devil is the devourer. Understanding—*comprehendere* —is likewise a devouring. Understanding swallows you up. . . . Understanding is a fearfully binding power, at times a veritable murder of the soul as soon as it flattens out vitally important differences. The core of the individual is a mystery of life, which is snuffed out when it is "grasped." That is why symbols want to be mysterious; they are not so merely because what is at the bottom of them cannot be clearly apprehended. . . . With our patients "analytical" understanding has a wholesomely destructive effect, like a corrosive or thermocautery, but is banefully destructive on sound tissue. It is technique we have learnt from the devil, always destructive, but useful where destruction is necessary. But one can commit no greater mistake than to apply the principles of this technique to an analysed psychology. More than that, all understanding in general, which is a conformity with general points of view, has the diabolical element in it and kills. It is a wrenching of another life out of its own course, forcing it into a strange one in which it cannot live. Therefore, in the later stages of analysis, we must help people towards those hidden and unlockable symbols, where the germ lies hidden like the tender seed in the hard shell.

True understanding seems to be one which does not understand, yet lives and works.[4]

This letter not only reveals the glories and the limits of psychological exploration, it also places all scientific and theological exploration in a humbling context. What a sacrifice is enshrined in this letter! What a quiet waiting on mystery is enjoined on the would-be explorer. What a judgment it is on those who profess and call themselves Christians. The friend of the soul veils his "eyes chastely before the mystery of the other," and both move beyond mere understanding (in the conceptual sense of the word) to mutual acceptance in the loving incomprehensibility of God.

Neither Ray Bradbury's parable nor Jung's letter should, therefore, terrify us into inactivity. Humility and sacrifice lead neither to retreat and spiritual paralysis nor to intellectual laziness. The parable and the letter are not only warnings concerning the stifling power of the mind and imagination in their desire to give some shape and order to human experience; they are also clues to the proper and creative approach to life's mysteries. Because we cannot know everything does not mean that we cannot know something.

Because we cannot do everything does not mean that we cannot do something. The danger of accepting our limitations with regard to what we can know and what we can do is that it could lead us into trivializing everything with the result that uncertainty, instability, and inactivity become virtues.

We are still the *ecclesia militans*, the Church Militant. We are an army requiring great acts of sacrifice from a new generation of heroes and heroines. What are we fighting? We are, as we have seen, fighting the devilish reductionisms that impoverish and undermine human existence. We oppose "final solutions" to any human problem because, as recent history has taught us, final solutions lead to the extermination of those who cannot be held or absorbed by the dominant group. We fight those tendencies which cannot tolerate the mystery and openness of human existence, and which seek to understand us and hence devour us. Christian companions are fellow soldiers in a battle to keep human life human. My companions keep passion—and the Passion—alive in me.

Human life is worthless, empty, hopeless without sacrifice at its heart. We live in an age and in a time when the quality of life has been so seriously eroded that on many parts of the planet we can hardly say that human life is human at all. The fire has gone out for many people. Many are as good as dead, in fact they might just as well be dead. Some of us, too, feel that way. The fire of the Spirit, the fire of religious faith, which has maintained and enlarged and stretched human beings for centuries, has been dampened, has been seriously diminished in the hearts of thousands of men and women. We find it hard to relate to one another as friends let alone as friends of the soul.

People come to church Sunday by Sunday. In some places the fire has gone out: There is no spark. There is no flame. There is nothing that enhances, stretches, and stimulates human life to keep it human. There is nothing that fosters the *extensio animi ad magna*. In some places the flame burns with frightening and uncontrollable energy. Yet the great function of the Body of Christ is nothing less than to set the world ablaze with the love which transfigures human life so that it becomes more and more glorious, more and more human, more and more delightful! Human life requires sacrifice at its heart. Without it life is dehumanized. The pursuit of happiness, the pursuit of pleasure for tiny, shriveled egos, the pursuit of mere ego gratification leads us, in the end, to the brink of the deepest possible despair. Why? Because we have yet to find our identity in God to answer that question "Who am I?" with Thomas Merton's ringing affirmation. "Who am I? My deepest realization of who I am is that I am one loved by Christ."

The gospel calls us home to ourselves and proclaims that we exist only in relation, that we do not belong to ourselves. We belong to Another. If we are to be human and stay human, we are to exist in relation to the One who made us and the One who loves us. This relationship to God is at the heart of what it is to be a human being. This is where the fire is. This is where the sacrifice is: To exist in relation to the living God is sacrificial. Every human love, every human relationship has suffering in it as well as delight. If human life is to be worthwhile, it has to have commitment. It has to have fire, and the fires necessary for our survival are in danger of going out. Spiritual companionship is concerned with the fire and its maintenance.

Our call as Christians is to live from the loving sacrifice at the heart of reality: our gospel proclaims that this sacrifice exists in the very heart of God himself. In the heart of God there is suffering love which draws us to himself, which calls us to engage with the world in creative suffering for the sake of its transformation. This is the divine Self-Emptying. Thus, the sacrificial center of our faith is the cross, where God shows himself as the One who is broken for us. The secret of human existence is revealed to us in the crucifixion and it is this: We are to be dispossessed of all things (to be dispossessed of our ambition, of our prejudices, of all the things we have accumulated) in order that we may possess all things in the power of the Spirit. This is why the author of the Epistle of Saint Peter calls us a royal priesthood. The human race is the community which offers sacrifice, thus all humanity is a priesthood. To be human is to be inherently priestly, but Christian companionship has a special priestly character. It makes explicit what is implicit in our humanity.

What is a priest? A priest is one who offers sacrifice; a priest is one who guards the flame; a priest is the one who sees the whole of creation as the theater of God's activity. And knows that it therefore is not to be exploited or abused, but to be reverenced. A priest is one who refuses to acquiesce to the terrible reductionism of human life, to reduce trees, animals, and plants—let alone human beings—to mere biochemistry, to mere physics, to mere biology. We claim that there is a Spirit energizing this creation, and that Spirit we dare call holy; that Spirit we dare identify with our Lord and Savior Jesus Christ. In his power we fight against reductionisms. You are not merely—what? an old and disillusioned man who will die soon, or a middle-aged woman stuck with a job and desperately wanting to get out, or a young person feeling the fire in the belly begin to grow cold. You may be any of these. Death, panic, or disillusionment may be near for you, but you are not just that. I, for one, cannot give a full account of my dog, let alone another human being who confronts me as a mystery, who, yes, is marked for death, but, because of the fire of the Spirit with which he was born, is also destined for something beyond death. The priesthood of humanity fights against our giving-in to these reductionisms. You are not just someone who is part of the "cycle of dung and death." You are destined for something beyond your dying, and that destination is part of who you are right now, however old you are, however cynical you may have become, however diminished that flame may be within you. You are destined for God. To be human is to understand our destiny in him.

This has concrete implications for our social and political life, because everyone we meet harbors that destiny within him or herself. We cherish it within us however deeply hidden that flame may be. There is a rabbinic saying: "Every human being is preceded by a legion of angels crying 'Make way for the image of God.' " It is very hard to believe that this is true in New York City, or London, or in any great city in the world. It is very hard in a city like New York, which has many dispossessed, many broken examples of humanity, to understand that human beings are the lively images of the One God. They are our brothers and sisters. They have within them too the terrific thing. The flame of humanity is as vital for them as it is for us if we are to keep human life human. Spiritual direction, in this context, takes on a new dimension. In pointing to the priestly character of all human beings, it can never be reduced to two people escaping from the world to indulge in a little private spiritual horticulture.

A priest is a sign of *transcendence*, a sign that there is always *more*. I am more than just this hulk which is going to die. I am more than a matter of conception, birth, and death. I am also a challenge, a summons, and a decision. I am not automatically a human being. I have to decide to be human; I have to decide to be human every day of my life. I have to decide to embrace the sacrificial priesthood of humanity. I have to decide to cooperate with the flame of the Spirit within me. The flame can become smaller and smaller and smaller until there is almost nothing left of what I might call a human being. God has so structured reality that he invites me to cooperate with him in my own creation and decide to be human, decide to be priestly, and that decision has to be conscious. My spiritual companion and guide constantly reminds me of the importance and necessity of that decision.

A priest, then, is a sign of transcendence, a sign that there is more to a human being than we see on the surface. A priest is also a sign of *tradition*. A tradition is that which hands on life. We are bearers of fire. What are we going to hand on to the next generation? What do we hand on to our children? Do we hand on a life without commitment? Do we hand on a life which is not marked by the keeping of promises? Do we hand on a life of lost integrity? Or do we hand on a life pregnant with promise because it is God's? Do we hand on a life full of hope because the future is God's? Do we hand on fire? There is a great deal at stake in our understanding ourselves as men and women of tradition, in this lively sense. We are those who are called to hand on life. Fire is very dangerous. The flame of God's love will burn us before it transforms us. Our God is a consuming fire. We will be burned up by either the fire of God's love or the fire of our self-centeredness. Which will it be? What is it in me that requires burning? What needs to be burnt up? What anxiety? What prejudice? What fear? What pettiness? What small-mindedness needs to be burnt? What is it that stops us from living? What is it that holds us back and makes us members of the living dead?

The flame is already present within us, and we are invited on a journey in the Spirit to get in touch with the flame again. There is within each human being the inner testimony, the inner witness of the Holy Spirit, who says, "You are known and loved and accepted.

The most real thing about you is the Holy Spirit. The terrific thing is there waiting to be discovered. You may be neurotic; you may be mean; you may be miserly; you may be a whole kettle of horrors, but the most real thing about you is the Holy Spirit because you are the dwelling place of God. You are the Temple of the Holy Spirit.[5] That means that we do not have to be diminished by other people's definitions of us, or worse, our own definition of ourselves as unworthy or as ugly or as unacceptable. At our very, very deepest, there is the Spirit of God calling us. The sad thing is that so many of us are rather like the blacksmith who had everything: a marvelous forge, anvils, hammers, tools—absolutely first-class equipment. He had everything except fire. We must have fire if we are to move and grow.

Saint Ignatius Loyola gave his followers this stunning command: "Go and set everything aflame." We are invited to be on fire with the Holy Spirit. Why? Because millions of people are dying of cold. The cold sets in when the sacrificial flame at the heart of things begins to die out.

We are invited in the power of the Spirit to warm this cold world back to life. We dare do this, not because of our own virtue or our own strength, but because the most real thing about us is the Holy Spirit. We are nothing less than the dwelling place of God, the Temple of the Holy Spirit. Death is not the end for us. In the power of the Spirit, we are sustained through that final bankruptcy. That is why we live in hope, that is why the fire within us can transform the world. That is why we dare to be Christians. To be a Christian is to be committed to the renewal of the world.

The risks of renewal are great, but we must take them. An evangelism fed by the fire of contemplation is a real power of the Holy Spirit. It is a union of contemplative life with apostolic mission. Effective evangelism comes only from those who know that outward action flows from an inner vision, and that vision sees the oppressive power of political and social structures as well as the pettiness that enslaves individuals. Saint John of the Cross speaks of the contemplative preacher: "What we have joyously harvested with the sickle of contemplation in solitude, we must thresh on the floor of preaching, and so broadcast." In the end this is what Christian companionship is for. It is for mission. It is for renewal.

Genuine revival requires the marriage of the contemplative with the prophetic. Only then will there be the kind of balance in which the full Word of God can break out with its healing power. The flame always needs to be pure of fanaticism and hatred. The inner work of prayer and the confrontation and nurture in spiritual companionship are a vital means of this purification.

The recovery of the art of spiritual direction, understood as that which takes account of the forming of the Christian community in the power of the Spirit, is an encouraging sign that the evangelical thrust of the Church's life will go forward on a sound basis. With proper spiritual foundations the Church cannot help but have a missionary identity. Evangelism must be rooted in a community, and unless that community is continually being formed in and by the Holy Spirit, there is no ground from which the gospel can be proclaimed.

My friend and former associate, Sister Rachel of the Episcopal Order of St. Helena, had a dream which illuminates the problem and the glory of evangelism: There was a great mail order catalog (like Sears or Montgomery Ward) from which you could order Jesus by mail. Jesus came in two kinds: one in a long red robe, with long curly blonde hair; the other in a long blue robe, with long curly brown hair. You could send off for the Jesus of your choice. There was, however, a catch. You never got what you ordered. Instead, you got the real thing! That's good news. The real thing, the terrific thing, comes to me in many ways. It comes through reading scripture and entering the drama of the liturgy. It also comes through the touch of a friend. It comes in the silence which holds friends together in Christ.

Saint John of the Cross wrote: "The Father utters one Word. That Word is his son, and he utters him forever in everlasting silence; and in silence the soul has to hear him."

The deep battles of the soul are conducted in silence. Silence understands sacrifice. And spiritual direction understands the power of an adoring silence which is shared with another. It is in the silence that I share with others that I begin to take delight in who I am.

Who am I? My deepest realization of who I am is that I am one loved by Christ. And who I am and who I am becoming is both a call to sacrifice and a source of great delight.

Epilogue
For the Hatching of the Heart

> Zen teaches nothing; it merely enables us to wake up and become more aware. It does not teach, it points. . . . The acts and gestures of a Zen Master are no more "statements" than is the ringing of an alarm clock.[1]
>
> *Thomas Merton*

A Christian companion helps me to grow by waking me up, by making me more aware. Sometimes it takes a great explosion to wake me up, but most of the time the teaching I receive from my friends is subtle and indirect. Little things teach me deep truths. I have, for example, been awakened to things inside myself by having to share a bathroom with four other people. The disproportionate rage I experience when I get out of the shower and find that my towel has disappeared teaches me a great deal about myself!

The world is something shared. This shared reality makes some form of companionship not only desirable but necessary. Christian companionship is often the alarm clock that wakes me up to the fact that my life is rooted in God who reveals himself as friend. We have seen that friendship is a much tougher and more resilient relationship than is often supposed. It involves, if necessary, the laying down of one's life, the willingness to suffer for another. It is the art of giving oneself away. It also involves dedication, discipline, and focused intention.

I have used many images in the book to describe what it means to be committed to Christian companionship—images of battle, pilgrimage, and sacrifice. All these images have a double quality about them in that they are characterized by both struggle and hope. It is very important to hold fast to the greater truths which are affirmed in Christian hope: the battle has been won; the pilgrimage begins and ends in God; sacrifice is for the sake of joy and delight.

My tendency has always been to stress the struggle at the expense of the hope, and a friend recently set off one of those alarm clocks which woke me up. We had been talking about the dark side of things and I said, "To light a candle is to cast a shadow" (a phrase I'd taken from Ursula Le Guin). My friend said, "Isn't that just like you! We don't light a candle in order to cast a shadow. We light a candle so that we can see." This response rang in my head and woke me up to the fact that I tend to emphasize the lesser things (the struggle) at the expense of the greater (the hope). When we light a candle, we must take the shadows seriously but not lose sight of the primary purpose of the candle.

Graham Greene's gloomy catholicism is always overcast by clouds. He is able to write about the muddy and ambiguous character of human interaction. Greeneland is shadowy. His vision, which I believe is alarmingly accurate at times, needs the corrective of a hopeful catholicism.

Compare and contrast the content and tone of Graham Greene and Father Thomas Keating. Both writers are saying something important about the Christian experience. Graham Greene writes:

> In the years between *The Heart of the Matter* and *The End of the Affair* I felt myself used and exhausted by the victims of religion. The vision of faith as an untroubled sea was lost forever; faith was now more like a tempest in which the lucky were engulfed and lost, and the unfortunate survived to be flung battered and bleeding along the shore. A better man could have found a life's work on the margin of that cruel sea, but my own course of life gave me no confidence in any aid I might proffer. I had no apostolic mission, and the cries for spiritual assistance maddened me because of my impotence. What was the Church for but to aid these sufferers? What was the priesthood for? I was like a man without medical knowledge in a village stricken with plague.[2]

Thomas Keating affirms that on the other side of the suffering is the sheer vulnerability of the love of God.

> The criterion of true Christian spirituality, affirmed by the gospel
> over and over again, is the practical and concrete love of neigh-
> bor which leads us to make the sacrifice of our own desires,
> convenience, and comfort, in order to meet the needs of others.
> Christ's commandment goes even further: "Love one another as
> *I have loved you*." (John 15:12). The love of Christ manifested
> itself in his sheer vulnerability. . . . Divine love is sheer vulnera-
> bility. . . . Being vulnerable means loving one another as Christ
> loved us.[3]

Keating's candle illuminates the darker corners of Greene's world.
Thus, two more images have crept in to describe certain aspects of
Christian companionship: the alarm clock and the candle. Friends
of my soul wake me up and light the way. Frederick Buechner in
his novel *Godric* presents me with a crowning image that gathers
together all the images of companionship which I have explored in
the previous pages.

> "When a man leaves home, he leaves behind some scrap of his
> heart. Is it not so, Godric?". . .
> "It's the same with a place a man is going to," he said. "only
> then he sends a scrap of his heart ahead."[4]

We are men and women with scattered and fragmented hearts.
I have left parts of myself behind with family and friends in places
which I scarcely remember. The friend of my soul is the one who
guards and honors these bits and pieces which I call "me." I have
also sent fragments ahead of myself and God knows where they are.
My friend knows of them and walks with me towards them. My
heart is on its way home and I have placed it in the keeping of
others, for it is only with them that I can find my way home. This
companionship is the setting of my social and political life as well
as my private and personal one. The belief that we are all fellow
pilgrims and companions has far-reaching social and political implications. Friendship has a public side, especially Christian friendship which is for the healing of the world. God is friendship and
this means that we are called to be friends in him. Not that we can
be close friends with millions of people across the earth. We can,
however, share in the friendliness of God and thereby build up the
network of interconnections which bind God's friends together.

And what is it all for? Again we find a clue in *Godric:*

> "Oh thou who art the sparrow's friend . . . have mercy on this
> world that knows not even when it sins. O holy dove, descend and
> roost on Godric here so that a heart may hatch in him at last.
> Amen."[5]

Companionship is for the hatching of our hearts. It is for the bring-
ing home of our scattered and fragmented selves, for the making
of a heart at home with itself. When I am truly at home with myself
in God, I can then be truly present to my friends and fellow
pilgrims.

It is all very simple. Companionship is your hand stretched out
to me when I am frozen and lost. It is the film of sweat between
pressed cheeks. It is your seeing in me *the terrific thing.* It is my
waiting attentively on your hurt and listening to your fears. It is the
tears, the laughter and the joy we share *in the Lord.* It is walking
together the way of the cross and living together in the power of
the resurrection. In short God's life is our life.

Notes

Preface

1. Peter Brook, *The Empty Space* (1968; reprint ed., Middlesex: Pelican-Penguin Books, 1972), p. 65.
2. Clement of Alexandria, "The Rich Man's Salvation" in *Clement of Alexandria*, ed. G. W. Butterworth (New York: G. P. Putnam's Sons, 1919), p. 355.
3. V. A. Demant in *Dictionary of Christian Ethics*, ed. John Macquarrie (Philadelphia: Westminster Press, 1967), p. 90.
4. Graham Greene, *Ways of Escape* (New York: Simon & Schuster, 1980).
5. A phrase from Tom Stoppard's play, *Jumpers*.
6. Aelred of Rievaulx, quoted in *Spiritual Friendship* (Kalamazoo, Mich.: Cistercian Publications, 1977).
7. Robert Coles, *Flannery O'Connor's South* (Baton Rouge: Louisiana State University Press, 1980), p. 159.
8. Greene, *Escape*, p. 159.
9. Coles, *South*, pp. 160–71.

Chapter 1

1. John Bunyan, *Pilgrim's Progress* (Middlesex: Penguin Books, 1965), pp. 93–94.
2. Editorial in *The Economist*, April 5, 1980, p. 7.
3. *The Economist* editorial, p. 7.
4 Aelred of Rievaulx, *Spiritual Friendship* (Kalamazoo, Mich.: Cistercian Publications, 1977), p. 51.
5. G. K. Chesterton, quoted in Dudley Barker, *G. K. Chesterton: A Biography* (Briarcliff Manor, NY: Stein & Day, 1973), p. 65.
6. Both reported in *The New York Times*. January 15, 1981, p. A 18.
7. Graham Greene, *Dr. Fischer of Geneva* (New York: Simon & Schuster, 1980), pp. 192–94.
8. Ibid., p. 192.
9. Ibid., p. 172.
10. Ibid., p. 193.

11. Paul Scott, *The Towers of Silence* (New York: Avon Books, 1979), p. 175.

12. Nikos Kazantzakis, *St. Francis of Assisi* (New York: Touchstone-Simon & Schuster, 1980).

Chapter 2

1. An image from Walker Percy, *The Second Coming* (New York: Farrar, Straus, and Giroux, 1980).

2. John Updike, *The Coup* (New York: Alfred A. Knopf, 1978).

3. See whole edition of *Saturday Review*, February 21, 1976, but particularly p. 23.

4. See Sheldon Kopp's two books, *Guru: Metaphors from a Psychotherapist* (Palo Alto: Science and Behavior Books, 1971) and *If You Meet the Buddha on the Road, Kill Him* (Palo Alto: Science and Behavior Books, 1972).

5. Kopp, *If You Meet the Buddha*, pp. 2–3.

6. Ibid., p. 4.

7. Ibid., p. 37.

8. Ibid., pp. 96–97.

9. William Johnston, *Silent Music* (New York: Harper & Row, Publishers, 1974), p. 121.

10. George Brown, *Synthesis I* (Redwood City, CA: The Synthesis Press, 1974), p. 39.

Chapter 3

1. Jacob Needleman, ed., *The Sword of Gnosis* (Middlesex: Penguin Books, 1974), p. 20.

2. Sheldon B. Kopp, *If You Meet the Buddha on the Road, Kill Him* (Palo Alto: Science and Behavior Books, 1972).

3. Simone Weil, *Waiting on God* (London: Collins, Fontana Paperback, 1959), p. 34.

4. Johann Wolfgang von Goethe, *Wilhelm Meister* (1795), translated by Walter Kaufman, quoted in Mark C. Taylor's *Journeys to Selfhood: Hegel and Kierkegaard* (Berkeley: University of California Press, 1980), p. 87.

5. William MacNamara, *The Human Adventure* (Garden City, New York: Doubleday & Co., 1974).

6. John V. Taylor, *The Go-Between God: The Holy Spirit and the Christian Mission* (Philadelphia: Fortress Press, 1973), p. 243.

Chapter 4

1. Harry Williams, *Poverty, Chastity and Obedience* (London: Mitchell Beazley, 1975), pp. 43–44.
2. Ibid., p. 49.
3. Ibid., p. 56.
4. Ibid., p. 56.
5. Ibid., p. 59.
6. Ibid., pp. 61–62.
7. Ibid., p. 68.
8. Ibid., p. 79.
9. Ibid., p. 79.
10. Ibid., p. 93.
11. Charles Williams, *The Greater Trumps* (New York: Pellegrini and Cudahy, 1950), p. 193.

Chapter 5

1. Augustine, *Confessions*, trans. with an introduction by R. S. Pine-Coffin (Middlesex: Penguin Books, 1961), p. 140.
2. Meister Eckhart in *Meister Eckhart: Selected Treatises and Sermons*, ed. J. M. Clark and J. V. Skinner (London: Faber & Faber, 1958), p. 93.
3. See John of the Cross, *The Collected Works of John of the Cross*, trans. Kieran Kavanaugh, O.C.D. and Otilio Rodriguez, O.C.D. and with introductions by Kieran Kavanaugh, O.C.D. (Washington: ICS Publications, 1973), especially his *Living Flame* for references to the role of spiritual direction. See p. 621 ff.
4. See also John of the Cross, *The Collected Works of John of the Cross, The Ascent of Mt. Carmel*, p. 70–71, and *The Dark Night of the Soul*, p. 312.
5. See St. Francis de Sales, *Introduction to the Devout Life*, ed. and trans. John K. Ryan (Garden City, New York: Image-Doubleday, 1955), especially pp. 164–79 on friendship. See also pp. 41–43 on the necessity of a guide.
6. Peter Salvin and Serenus Cressy, *The Life of Fr. Augustine Baker, O.S.B.*, ed. Dom Justin McCann, O.S.B. (London: Burns & Oates, 1933), p. 92–93.
7. Dom Augustine Baker, *Holy Wisdom*, ed. J. Norbert Sweeney, O.S.B. (London: Burns and Oates, 1876), p. 35.
8. Ibid., p. 85.

Chapter 6

1. David Baily Harned, *Images for Self-Recognition: The Christian as Player, Sufferer, and Vandal* (New York: The Seabury Press, 1977), p. 2.
2. William Golding, *Darkness Visible* (London: Faber & Faber, 1979).

3. Walker Percy, *The Second Coming* (New York: Farrar, Straus, and Giroux, 1980), p. 123.

4. Richard Sennett, *Authority* (New York: Alfred A. Knopf, 1980), p. 16.

5. Ibid., p. 76.

6. Ibid., p. 8.

7. Michael Foucault, *Discipline and Punishment*, quoted in Sennett, *Authority*, p. 92.

8. Sennett, *Authority*, p. 129.

9. Ibid., p. 129.

10. Ibid., p. 129.

11. Ibid., p. 132.

12. See Sennett, *Authority*, p. 142 ff.

13. Percy, *Second Coming*, p. 181.

14. See Harned, *Self-Recognition*, p. 54 ff.

15. Ibid., p. 65.

16. Jacob Needleman, *A Sense of the Cosmos* (New York: E. P. Dutton, 1977), pp. 13–14.

17. Carl Gustav Jung, *Memories, Dreams, Reflections* (New York: Pantheon Books, 1963), p. 192 ff.

18. From an unpublished paper by Barbara Hannah, "The Active Imagination."

19. From Hannah.

Chapter 7
1. Ernest Becker, *The Denial of Death* (New York: Free Press, 1973), p. 80.

2. This section and what follows owe a great deal to an unpublished essay by R. A. Norris, *Hunting the Transcendent*.

3. Ibid.

4. This section owes a great deal to James Hillman's *The Dream and the Underworld* (New York: Colophon-Harper & Row, 1979).

5. Ibid., p. 65.

6. Teilhard de Chardin, *Le Milieu Divin* (Paris, 1957; rpt. London: Fontana-Collins, 1964), p. 72.

7. Ibid., p. 72.

8. Walker Percy, *The Second Coming* (New York: Farrar, Straus, and Giroux, 1980), pp. 272–73.

9. Charles Williams, *The Figure of Beatrice: A Study in Dante* (1961; rpt. New York: Octagon-Farrar, Straus, and Giroux, 1972), p. 147.

10. Simone Weil, *Waiting on God*, trans. Emma Craufurd (Paris, 1950; rpt. London: Fontana-Collins, 1959), p. 152 ff. See whole section on friendship, p. 152–160.

11. Ibid., p. 152.

Chapter 8

1. Carl Gustav Jung, *Letters*, ed. Gerhard Adler and Anelia Jaffe, trans. R. F. C. Hull (Princeton: Princeton University Press, 1973), see f.n. 8, Vol. I, p. 19.

2. Raimundo Panikkar, ed. and trans., *The Vedic Experience: Mantramanjari* (Berkeley: University of California Press, 1977), pp. 51–52.

3. See Robert J. Daly, S. J., *The Origins of the Christian Doctrine of Sacrifice* (London: Darton Longman and Todd, 1978).

4. From Ray Bradbury, "The God in Science Fiction," in *Saturday Review*, December 10, 1977.

5. Carl Gustav Jung. *Letters*, ed. Gerhard Adler and Anelia Jaffe, trans. R. F. C. Hull (Princeton: Princeton University Press, 1973), Vol. I, Letter of 6 November 1915, p. 30–31.

Epilogue

1. Thomas Merton, *Zen and the Birds of Appetite*, (New York: New Directions Books, 1963), pp. 49–50. (Merton is quoting D. T. Suzuki.)

2. Graham Greene, *Ways of Escape* (New York: Simon & Schuster, 1980), p. 261.

3. Thomas Keating, *The Heart of the World* (New York: Crossroad Books, 1981), p. 13.

4. Frederick Buechner, *Godric* (New York: Atheneum, 1980), pp. 36–37.

5. Ibid., p. 38.